AF173224

Changing Communities in Challenging Contexts to Address Intimate Partner Violence

Lori K. Sudderth

Changing Communities in Challenging Contexts to Address Intimate Partner Violence

Doing the Impossible

palgrave
macmillan

Lori K. Sudderth
Criminal Justice Program
Quinnipiac University
Cheshire, CT, USA

ISBN 978-3-031-75355-8   ISBN 978-3-031-75356-5   (eBook)
https://doi.org/10.1007/978-3-031-75356-5

© The Editor(s) (if applicable) and The Author(s), under exclusive license to Springer Nature Switzerland AG 2024

This work is subject to copyright. All rights are solely and exclusively licensed by the Publisher, whether the whole or part of the material is concerned, specifically the rights of translation, reprinting, reuse of illustrations, recitation, broadcasting, reproduction on microfilms or in any other physical way, and transmission or information storage and retrieval, electronic adaptation, computer software, or by similar or dissimilar methodology now known or hereafter developed.
The use of general descriptive names, registered names, trademarks, service marks, etc. in this publication does not imply, even in the absence of a specific statement, that such names are exempt from the relevant protective laws and regulations and therefore free for general use.
The publisher, the authors and the editors are safe to assume that the advice and information in this book are believed to be true and accurate at the date of publication. Neither the publisher nor the authors or the editors give a warranty, expressed or implied, with respect to the material contained herein or for any errors or omissions that may have been made. The publisher remains neutral with regard to jurisdictional claims in published maps and institutional affiliations.

Cover illustration: © John Rawsterne/patternhead.com

This Palgrave Macmillan imprint is published by the registered company Springer Nature Switzerland AG
The registered company address is: Gewerbestrasse 11, 6330 Cham, Switzerland

If disposing of this product, please recycle the paper.

Acknowledgments

This book is dedicated to the hundreds of survivors of intimate partner violence who have spoken to me about the abuse, their recovery, and their resilience in the context of geography, rurality, poverty, and identity. It is also dedicated to the inspirational work of the staff of organizations around the world that facilitate and fund programs that support these women in their journey to wholeness and endeavor to make life better for the next generation. I would like to acknowledge the work of Raise Your Voice Saint Lucia, Inc., the New Haven/León Sister City Project, the Women's Justice Initiative, and Rockflower for the tremendous contributions they make to empowering women and ending gender-based violence.

In particular, I am grateful to Catherine Sealys, Theresa Peter, and Souyenne Hackshaw for their insight and patience with my questions. I also would like to thank Erendira Vanegas for introducing me to the women of Goyena and helping me to see their perspective. My understanding of victim advocacy and Maori culture benefited from myriad conversations with Dr. Annabel Taylor. I also learned so much from my conversations with Tine Ward of Rockflower, Dr. Mary Catherine Driese of the Women's Justice Initiative, and Dr. Janie Leatherman of Fairfield University.

CONTENTS

CHAPTER 1

Introduction: Community, Battering, and Safety

Abstract This chapter provides the theoretical and practical backdrop for the challenges of responding to intimate partner violence in low-income countries, particularly in communities where anonymity is low, and identity or emotional support is inextricably connected to family and friends. Relevant literature on intimate partner violence, the role of community, criminal justice, and feminist initiatives are reviewed. The limitations of formal responses to intimate partner violence in these settings, such as rural areas, small islands, and tribal communities, are discussed as well.

Keywords Intimate partner violence · Domestic violence · Violence against women · Community · Low-income countries · Formal support · Informal support · Rural · Island · Tribal · Feminist · Criminal justice response

In 2014, I crossed the border into Nogales, Mexico with a colleague to interview immigrants who had been deported from the United States after crossing illegally into the United States. Our first stop was a breakfast served in a tent by the Kino Border Initiative, a Jesuit-funded effort to support deportees with a hot meal, clothes, and medical attention. Immigrants in this category are almost all men seeking work, but women

© The Author(s), under exclusive license to Springer Nature Switzerland AG 2024
L. K. Sudderth, *Changing Communities in Challenging Contexts to Address Intimate Partner Violence*,
https://doi.org/10.1007/978-3-031-75356-5_1

also brave the desert to get to the United States, in some cases, escaping gender-based violence in their home country (Rosenblum, Gibson, and Leong 2022). In fact, I picked up a memorial picture of 14-year-old Josseline Jamileth Hernandez Quinteros from El Salvador, who crossed the border with her younger brother in 2008. She died of dehydration during the crossing, and her grief-stricken brother eventually made his way back to collect her remains. I keep her picture at my desk when I am writing, a reminder of the obstacles women in low-income countries face as they try to find the safety and security that I take for granted.

Our second stop was a KBI-sponsored shelter for women deportees, and we spoke to some of the women about their experiences. Most came from small villages with few opportunities for employment; some were hoping to join family, husbands in the United States, carrying young children with them. I asked about the options for women in abusive relationships in those villages, and the response was that abused wives have three choices: (1) find a woman in another village who will take them in, (2) leave/immigrate far away from family and friends to get away from the abusive spouse, or (3) put up with the abuse. A year and a half later, I was visiting a small, rural village in Nicaragua, and I heard about these same options (E. Vanegas,[1] personal communication, April 15, 2012). In this village, however, after an educational program on violence against women and civil rights, one woman had, indeed, opened her home to any women fleeing intimate partner violence.

These stories kindled my curiosity about the role of small, under-resourced communities as refuge from violence and the effects of programming; one woman was literally sheltering victims of spousal violence or offering emotional support to endure unchecked abuse, and in the process, challenging the gendered expectations that fueled the violence in the first place. Later, on the board of the non-profit organization serving this rural area in Nicaragua, I began reading and writing about the possibilities of social change on the community level to address gender-based violence in places where resources are limited and identity is inextricably linked to location through family, friends, tradition, or simply familiarity (Ellsberg et al. 2001; Salazar et al. 2012; Sudderth 2020). It occurred to me that all the rural areas I had visited shared these challenges

---

[1] Erendira Vanegas was a social worker in Leon, Nicaragua, and she spoke with the author about her program on domestic violence for the women of Goyena, a small rural village outside of Leon.

with survivors living on small islands, in tribal communities, and even on small college campuses.

In some ways, these contexts—islands, small towns/rural areas, and tribal communities should be places where intimate partner violence is less likely to happen. They are places where people tend to know each other; it is almost impossible to be anonymous and unnoticed. These social connections decrease the likelihood of isolation, which is one of the driving risk factors for intimate partner violence (Lanier and Maume 2009). But tribal communities often have higher rates of intimate partner violence than non-tribal communities (e.g., Perry 2022); in rural areas, the challenge of responding to intimate partner violence includes the fact that everyone knows everyone else; and on small islands, escape from an abusive relationship is hindered by geography and the pull of close-knit family and friendship ties (Andrew 2020; Sudderth 2013).

INTIMATE PARTNER VIOLENCE

Intimate partner violence (IPV) is defined as "any behaviour within an intimate relationship that causes physical, psychological or sexual harm to those in the relationship," including physical violence, emotional abuse, sexual violence, and controlling behaviors (World Health Organization 2012: 1). Around the world, the lifetime rate of intimate partner violence ranges from 13 to 61% of ever-partnered women (Garcia-Moreno, Jansen, Ellsberg, Heise, and Watts 2005). There have been efforts to standardize the measurement of IPV as the percentage of women in a population who have experienced "physical or sexual violence by current or former partner during the last year" or "during lifetime" (Friends of the Chair of the United Nations Statistical Commission 2008: 3). Cepeda, Lacalle-Calderon, and Torralba (2021) created an index to measure violence against women, which included intimate partner violence, in 102 countries, using measures of physical violence, sexual violence, psychological violence, and economic violence. Countries were ranked as low, medium, high, and very high in violence against women. For example, as a region, Latin America and the Caribbean ranked in the medium range, although Honduras, Guatemala, Belize, and Mexico were listed as either high or very high on the index. Nicaragua and Jamaica were both in the medium range. In other words, although IPV is detected in every nation around the world, there are dramatic variations in the extent of the problem between regions and across countries.

Intimate partner violence is theorized as both a product of patriarchy as well as a way of reinforcing the patriarchal privileges of men (Ahrens 2006; DeKeseredy and Schwartz 2013; Edwards et al. 2011; Ullman 2010; Walby 1990). Even though intimate partner violence is outlawed in many countries, and a human rights violation internationally (Merry 2009), it is still considered normative in places where, often, women have the least ability to resist it. Reliance on sanctions to stop IPV means waiting for the violence to happen and then responding to a behavior that is illegal but culturally normative (Lundgren 1998). Because of the complex set of predictors driving IPV, UN Women and several other organizations recognize that prevention is key to stopping IPV, but there is disagreement on what works and how to juggle individual and community-level programming to change attitudes and behavior.

Victims of intimate partner violence, therefore, make choices within a social structure that values men over women, unequally distributes resources, allows varying access to firearms, and offers shifting social stability and legal protection (Iadicola and Shupe 2003; Krug et al. 2002; Leatherman 2011; Nikolic-Ristanovic 2000). In those places where identity is tied to a colonialist past, the community is a place of refuge from structural violence. Leaving that community means escaping interpersonal violence to subject oneself to structural violence without the protective cape of family and friends (Manjoo 2011). Some of these barriers of structural violence may take precedence over escaping an abusive partner (e.g., Brush 2011). In larger, urban communities, anonymity is more easily achieved in that shelters are available, support groups, therapy, and transportation are more readily available for someone who wants to reconstruct themselves without a violent partner. In geographically limited communities, however, there is very little alternative space for safe refuge or even for discussion of gender restrictions. In small towns, tribal communities, and islands, the alternative space is in a place separate from the social networks that feed their attachment to family, place, and friends. As Price (2012) pointed out, rather than escape, the objective may be to change the community so that victims can find safety at home.

COMMUNITY AND INTIMATE PARTNER VIOLENCE

In the traditional sense, a community is a place where people share a location or some common experience that connects them to each other (e.g., Ritzer and Ryan 2010). Some research indicates it is not the place but the connectedness of a community that should be measured through its impact on physical and mental health (Collins et al. 2017). Social capital is defined as "links, shared values and understandings in society that enable individuals and groups to trust each other and so work together" (Organization for Economic Co-operation and Development [OECD] 2007: 102). Social capital is composed of *bonds* to others in the community, *bridges* to the extended community, and *linkages* to the hierarchy of the outside world (OECD 2007). Social capital is linked to trust and values, that people must feel a sense of safety and security in order to be a cohesive and connected group (OECD 2007). While these community linkages have deteriorated in some places like the United States (Putnam 2000), digital communities have evolved with the proliferation of the internet, telecommunications, and social media (OECD 2007).

In 1991, the controversial historian Elizabeth Fox-Genovese pointed out that feminists who described the community as oppressive to women also suggested that women derived emotional support from their strong bonds with the community. Survivors of intimate partner violence stand in the crossfires of that contradiction. Hooks (2001) suggested that most people in a community do not approve of male violence toward women, but they are more ambivalent about patriarchy and male privilege. Their community, composed of family, friends, neighbors, and coworkers, may be sources of emotional support and protection from an abusive spouse or reinforce the silence around gender-based violence and traditional gender restrictions (Baumgartner 1993; Stark 2007).

To change this situation, feminists have focused on international mechanisms, treaties, and conventions to pressure governments to outlaw violence against women, change women's status, and provide for the survivors of IPV with appropriate support. The Convention on the Elimination of All Forms of Discrimination against Women (CEDAW) includes two recommendations (12 and 19) that address violence against women. The first (No. 12) recommends that signatory states report how they are addressing violence against women, and the second, General recommendation No. 19, recognizes gender-based violence as discrimination and asks signatory states to collect information on violence and report it to the CEDAW Committee (United Nations 2003). A more recent effort is to pass an Optional Protocol to CEDAW making explicit that violence against women is unacceptable by clarifying expected standards of progress (EveryWomanTreaty 2018).

However, there are limitations to the top-down approach to addressing violence against women. The imposition of gender equality arouses suspicion among conservatives who argue that women are not equal to men, and among feminists who argue that the language of CEDAW leads to gender neutrality rather than addressing the special needs of women.[2] Even some signatories of CEDAW defend patriarchal practices in their countries as "cultural," minimal, or characteristic of marginalized communities, rather than structural inequalities—despite the fact that NGOs have successfully built on cultural practices to address violence against women (e.g., Samoa Women's Support Group 2024). In fact, there are few enforcement mechanisms for UN conventions other than international pressure to appear supportive of human rights (See Merry 2006). Moreover, international standards are most effective when they are translated into local language and programming, collaborative, and intersectional (Mathonsi and Tallis 2022; Merry 2006).

In addition, Mathonsi and Tallis (2022) point out that the feminism of the global north is too narrow in its focus on men's power over women; they challenge international feminists to think in terms of intersectionality rather than the dichotomous power dynamics of males and females. According to Merry (2006), global feminist ideals and local practice can take different forms, including (a) the drafting of international statements on the appropriate legal and sociological response to violence against women, given the immense range of cultural interpretations; (b) programming and legal innovations in addressing violence against women, adapted from one setting to another, relying on international standards and ideas for direction; (c) local NGO representatives who attend international conferences on violence against women and human rights and then take what they learn back to their communities. This is not meant to diminish the need for international and state legislation to create better structural conditions for responding to IPV, but underscores the need for community practices that help to implement those principles.

---

[2] These arguments are reviewed in Merry's (2006) chapter on "Gender Violence and the CEDAW Process" in *Human Rights & Gender Violence.*

Community, Criminal Justice, and IPV

The criminal justice response to intimate partner violence in high-income countries like the United States, Australia, New Zealand, the United Kingdom, and Canada has improved dramatically over the last four decades, although there are still unanswered questions about the effectiveness of mandatory arrest, offender treatment, or policing technology to reduce recidivism or domestic violence murders (Przeszlowski, Guerette, and Sudderth 2023; Sherman 2018). The criminal justice response to violence against women still faces the challenge of a low reporting rate as well as barriers to victims continuing in the process through prosecution (Kilpatrick et al. 2007; Patterson and Campbell 2010). Nevertheless, in the global North, feminists argued that a man being abusive to his female partner should be considered no less serious than two men brawling in the streets, and thus requires a formal, punitive response; the lack of this level of response was linked to the protection of patriarchal privilege (e.g., Schechter 1982). In the United States, for example, this demand for arrest and prosecution of IPV charges followed a larger trend relying on formal control institutions to respond to criminal or deviant behavior in light of declining community connections (Putnam 2000).

Low-income countries often seek to adopt the policing models of wealthier nations to replicate their success in reducing intimate partner violence, but the policy transfer, is not a perfect fit (Maguire and King 2013; Snider 1998). Low-income countries may symbolically adopt policing practices or pass legislation that mirrors international standards, but fail to provide the training for officers to more effectively carry out the new response to the crime (Maguire and King 2013). In addition, the process of criminalizing IPV is a process of criminalizing violence that is culturally normalized, and thus, typically not taken seriously (Kelly and Radford 1998; Lundgren 1998; Merry 2006).

By the same token, intervening in the behavior of individuals who violate the law does not change the structural framework of society that grants men privileges that feed violence against women (Pease 2019). The reliance on criminal justice responses to IPV has also traditionally benefitted the more powerful members of society while exercising control over the less powerful (Pease 2019; Snider 1998). For example, Anderson, Gleckman-Krut, and Johnson (2018) show how sexual violence reinforces both gendered and racial hierarchies. Historically, criminal justice reforms addressing violence against women, which were advocated by white feminists, reinforced racial hierarchies by targeting African American men for prosecution (Gross et al. 2017), leaving African American women skeptical of the efficacy of the criminal justice approach in protecting them from sexual and physical violence (Crenshaw 2012). Similarly, relying on police to make arrests for IPV requires trust in law enforcement (Price 2012), a luxury often not available to IPV victims in low-income countries. Studies in low- and middle-income countries indicate that women who experience intimate partner violence, in fact, have little faith in law enforcement or in the courts, and often believe that reporting to them will make the situation worse (see Wood et al. 2021). Legal frameworks, in fact, may be set up to reinforce patriarchal privilege, rather than intervene in abusive relationships (Anderson et al. 2018; Arnull and Stewart 2021). The criminal justice response to crime, then, may end up reinforcing structural violence.

Survivors of IPV in low- and middle-income countries seldom seek formal assistance, which is not in and of itself unique to these settings (Garcia-Moreno et al. 2005). Financial dependence on a male partner, however, in combination with compelling patriarchal norms in small communities reinforce the tendency of intimate partner violence survivors to rely on family and friends instead of formal services (McCleary-Sills et al. 2016; Wood et al. 2021). In other words, community characteristics (e.g., proportion of women experiencing intimate partner violence, age at first marriage), in addition to individual-level characteristics (e.g., the number of controlling behaviors, increased severity of abuse, female employment) can depress or enhance IPV survivors' willingness to reach out for help (Hayes and Franklin 2017). Thus, programming that is focused on women's empowerment may challenge traditional gender restrictions and norms, but also encourage more disclosure of abuse (Hayes and Franklin 2017).

Safety planning is standard practice among domestic violence victim advocates, and it involves creating a plan for safety, depending on the individual victim's circumstances and needs (Davies et al. 1998). Safety planning represents a response to structural and interpersonal violence by empowering victims of IPV to seek support and to re-assert control over their lives as women and as survivors (Drumm 2007).

Within a rural context, survivors of intimate partner violence may seek assistance that is relatively random, informal rather than formal, and highly dependent upon social networks (Ellsberg et al. 2001; Salazar et al.

2012; Sudderth 2015; UN Women 2014). Safety planning in communities where anonymity and resources are low may, in fact, emphasize the incorporation of their social networks into the plan (Sudderth 2017). Price (2012) points out that violence against women can be viewed through a lens of "space" that women can safely occupy versus "space" they cannot. That safety is based on the structural, societal position of women and the obstacles and threats they negotiate and face as women. Coercive control constricts the space in which abused women feel safe, negatively impacting their mental health and social connections; escaping a controlling relationship has the opposite effect—enhancing mental health and reinforcing social connections (Sharp-Jeffs, Kelly, and Klein 2018). When survivors of intimate partner violence live in communities where they fear for their safety (e.g., due to violent crime in the area), they restrict their own activities outside the home, negatively impacting life satisfaction (Beeble, Sullivan, and Byee 2011), but also exacerbating the sense of limited safety.

In high-income countries, the approach to safety planning necessarily involved creating a refuge from the community of origin, which offered little support from the abuse (National Collective of Independent Women's Refuge 2012; Schechter 1982). Seeking help in the form of shelter is complicated by the normative loss experienced by women who leave their homes, neighborhoods, families, and friends to temporarily reside in a hidden location (Abrahams 2010; Goodman and Epstein 2008). For women from oppressed or marginalized communities, for women who have lived their lives in the comfort of small, rural communities or who have never known life beyond their island, the state or the criminal justice system or a distant shelter does not necessarily represent safety (DeKeseredy 2021; Smith 2006; Websdale 2001). Certainly, women's decisions to seek shelter revolve around children, the severity of the violence, but also employment, financial support, and distrust of authority (Dasgupta and Warrier 1996; DeKeseredy 2021; Gelles and Straus 1988; Horton and Johnson 1993; Smith 2006; Websdale 2001). In some communities, reporting a partner to the police would have worse consequences for the victim than the perpetrator (Ferraro 2006; Odero et al. 2014; Wood et al. 2021). In addition, for marginalized women, comfort, as well as a profound sense of who they are in the world comes from the family and friends around them and the culture that surrounds them all. To leave that community for refuge provided by an unknown organization, connected to a criminal justice system that is suspect or a government associated with that system, may not seem like a reasonable option. For women in marginalized or isolated communities, those connections are associated with protection in a way that the criminal justice system is not (Smith 2006; Websdale 2001). In a review of the research on safety planning in low- and middle-income countries, Wood, Glass, and Decker (2021) found that women in low- and middle-income countries actively engaged in safety planning by (a) disclosing to family and friends rather than authorities, (b) avoiding or preventing conflict with the abusive partner, often by conforming to traditional gender expectations, (c) tolerating the violence passively with the assumption that it would dissipate over time, and (d) accumulating financial resources to change the dynamics of the relationship or to leave.

Moreover, in smaller communities where people tend to know one another, victims of IPV may be living in close proximity with friends and family of the abusive partner. Both abusive partners and victims live within a cultural and structural context that influences the distribution of power, resources, and support, complicating a victim's exit strategy from and abusive relationship (Iadicola and Shupe 2003; Johnson 1995; Sanday 1981; Yllo and Straus 1991). Wood et al. (2021) point out that the limited literature on safety planning in low- and middle-income countries indicates a preference for staying in the relationship, perhaps based on a lack of choices, but also their preferences for informal sources of support and continuing in their relationships. The lack of support from law enforcement, the dearth of services for survivors, particularly in rural areas in low- and middle-income countries, and the economic dependence of women in these settings provide the context for decisions to strategize about safety without leaving the relationship (Wood et al. 2021).

These empirical findings are strikingly similar to the conversations I had with rural and migrant women from Central America, as well as other survivors from comparable contexts. This book is dedicated to these women and the teams of people around the world who work to take the ideals of international feminism and turn them into reality.

References

Abrahams, Hilary. 2010. Life after leaving: Examining long-term outcomes for women escaping domestic abuse. *Te Awatea Review* 8 (1&2): 4–8.

Ahrens, Courtney E. 2006. Being silenced: The impact of negative social reactions on the disclosure of rape. *American Journal of Community Psychology* 38: 63–274.

Anderson, Elizabeth A., Miriam Gleckman-Krut, and Lanora Johnson. 2018. Silence, power, and inequality: An intersectional approach to sexual violence. *Annual Review of Sociology* 44: 99–122.

Andrew, Jennan P. 2020. *Intimate partner violence in LBTQ relationships in Jamaica* [Master's thesis, Ohio University]. OhioLINK Electronic Theses and Dissertations Center. http://rave.ohiolink.edu/etdc/view?acc_num=ohi ou1585232198183695.

Arnull, Elaine, and Stacey Stewart. 2021. Developing a theoretical framework to discuss mothers experiencing domestic violence and being subject to interventions: A cross-national perspective. *International Journal for Crime, Justice and Social Democracy* 10 (2): 113–126.

Baumgartner, Mary Pat. 1993. Violent networks: The origins and management of domestic conflict. In *Aggression and violence*, ed. R.B. Felsen and J.T. Tedeschi, 209–231. Washington, D.C.: American Psychological Association.

Beeble, Marisa L., Cris M. Sullivan, and Deborah Bybee. 2011. The impact of neighborhood factors on the well-being of survivors of intimate partner violence over time. *American Journal of Community Psychology* 47 (3–4): 287–306.

Brush, Lisa D. 2011. *Poverty, battered women, and work in U.S. public policy.* New York City: Oxford University Press Inc.

Cepeda, Isabel, Maricruz Lacalle-Calderon, and Miguel Torralba. 2021. Measuring violence against women: A global index. *Journal of Interpersonal Violence* 37 (19–20): 1–25.

Collins, Jessica, Bernadette M. Ward, Pamela Snow, Sancra Kippen, and Fiona Judd. 2017. Compositional, contextual, and collective community factors in mental health and well-being in Australian rural communities. *Qualitative Health Research* 27 (5): 677–687.

Crenshaw, Kimberlé Williams. 2012. From private violence to mass incarceration: Thinking intersectionally about women, race, and social control. *UCLA Law Review* 59 (6): 1418–1472.

Dasgupta, Shamita Das, and Sujata Warrier. 1996. In the footsteps of 'Arundhati': Asian Indian women's experience of domestic violence in the United States. *Violence against Women* 2: 238–259.

Davies, Jill, Eleanor Lyon, and Diane Monti-Catania. 1998. *Safety planning with battered women: Complex lives/difficult choices.* Thousand Oaks: Sage Publications.

DeKeseredy, Walter S. 2021. *Woman Abuse in Rural Places.* New York City: Routledge.

DeKeseredy, Walter, and Martin Schwartz. 2013. *Male peer support and violence against women: The history and verification of a theory.* Boston: Northeastern University Press.

Drumm, J. 2007. *"Turning the tide: A national and local coordinated approach to addressing domestic violence in the United Kingdom."* Auckland, NZ: Preventing Violence in the Home. Retrieved 6 March 2014 from www.2sh ine.org.nz/library/Documents/turningthetide.pdf.

Edwards, Katie M., Christina M. Dardis, and Christine A. Gidycz. 2011. Women's disclosure of dating violence: A mixed methodological study. *Feminism & Psychology* 22 (4): 507–517.

Ellsberg, Mary Carroll, Anna Winkvist, Rodolfo Peña, and Henrik Stenlund. 2001. Women's strategic responses to violence in Nicaragua. *Journal of Epidemiology & Community Health* 55 (8): 547–555.

EveryWomanTreaty. 2018. *"Optional Protocol."* Retrieved 13 June 2024 at https://everywoman.org/optional-protocol/.

Ferraro, Kathleen. 2006. *Neither angels nor demons: Women, crime, and victimization.* Boston: Northeastern University Press.

Fox-Genovese, Elizabeth. 1991. *Feminism without illusions: A critique of individualism.* Chapel Hill & London: The University of North Carolina Press.

Friends of the Chair of the United Nations Statistical Commission. 2008. *Report of the Friends of the Chair of the United Nations Statistical Commission on the indicators on violence against women.* New York: Economic and Social Council.

Garcia-Moreno, Claudia, Henrica A.F.M.. Jansen, Mary Ellsberg, Lori Heise, and Charlotte Watts. 2005. *WHO multi-country study on women's health and domestic violence against women.* Geneva: World Health Organization.

Gelles, Richard J., and Murray A. Straus. 1988. *Intimate violence: The causes and consequences of abuse in the Family.* New York: Touchstone.

Goodman, Lisa A., and Deborah Epstein. 2008. *Listening to battered women: A survivor-centered approach to advocacy, mental health, and justice.* Washington: American Psychological Association.

Gross, Samuel R., Maurice Possley, and Klara Stephens. 2017. *"Race and wrongful convictions in the United States."* Retrieved 22 June 2022 at http://www.law.umich.edu/speical/exoneration/Documents/Race_and_Wrongful-Convictions.pdf.

Hayes, Brittany E., and Cortney A. Franklin. 2017. Community effects on women's help-seeking behaviour for intimate partner violence in India: Gender disparity, feminist theory, and empowerment. *International Journal of Comparative and Applied Criminal Justice* 41 (1–2): 79–94.

Hooks, Bell. 2001. *All about love: New visions.* New York City: HarperCollins Publishers.

Horton, Anne L., and Barry L. Johnson. 1993. Profile and strategies of women who have ended abuse. *Families in Society: The Journal of Contemporary Human Services* 74 (8): 481–492.

Iadicola, Peter, and Anson Shupe. 2003. *Violence, inequality, and human freedom*. Lanham, MD: Rowman & Littlefield Publishers Inc.

Johnson, Michael P. 1995. Patriarchal terrorism and commoncouple violence: Two forms of violence against women. *Journal of Marriage and the Family* 57: 283–294.

Kelly, Liz and Jill Radford. 1998. "Sexual violence against women and girls: An approach to an international overview." In *Rethinking violence against women*, eds. E. W. Dobash and R. P. Dobash, 53–76. Thousand Oaks: Sage Publicatons.

Kilpatrick, Dean G., Heidi S. Resnick, Kenneth J. Ruggiero, Lauren M. Conoscenti, and Jenna McCauley. 2007. "*Drug-facilitated, incapacitated, and forcible rape: A national study.*" Washington, D.C.: National Institute of Justice. NIJ report 2005-WG-BX0006.

Krug, Etienne G., Linda L. Dahlberg, James A. Mercy, Anthony B. Zwi, and R. Lozano. 2002. *World report on violence and health*. Geneva: World Health Organization.

Lanier, Christina, and Michael O. Maume. 2009. Intimate partner violence and social isolation across the rural/urban divide. *Violence against Women* 15 (11): 1311–1330.

Leatherman, Judith L. 2011. *Sexual violence and armed conflict*. Cambridge: Polity Press.

Lundgren, Eva. 1998. The hand that strikes and comforts: Gender construction and the tension between body and symbol. In *Rethinking violence against women*, ed. R.E. Dobash and R.P. Dobash, 169–198. Thousand Oaks: Sage Publications.

Maguire, Edward R., and William R. King. 2013. Transferring criminal investigation methods from developed to developing nations. *Policing & Society* 23 (3): 346–361.

Manjoo, Rashida 2011. *Report of the Special Rapporteur on violence against women, its causes and consequences. Human Rights Council, Seventeenth session*. New York: United Nations General Assembly.

Mathonsi, Claire, and Vicci Tallis. 2022. Feminist advocacy in Africa: Voices and actions. *Empowering Women for Gender Equity* 36 (3): 2–10.

McCleary-Sills, Jennifer, Sophi Namy, Joyce Nyoni, Datius Rweyemamu, Adrophina Salvatory, and Ester Steven. 2016. Stigma, shame and women's limited agency in help-seeking forintimate partner violence. *Global Public Health* 11 (1–2): 224–235.

Merry, Sally Engle. 2006. *Human rights and gender violence: Translating international law into local justice.* Chicago and London: University of Chicago Press.

Merry, Sally Engle. 2009. *Gender Violence: A Cultural Perspective.* Chichester: Wiley-Blackwell.

National Collective of Independent Women's Refuge. 2012. *Our story: Working for women past, present and future.* Retrieved Sept. 29, 2012 from https://womensrefuge.org.nz/WR/About-Us/Our-story.htm.

Nikolić-Ristanović, Vesna. 2000. *Women, violence and war: Wartime victimization of refugees in the balkans.* Budapest: Central European University Press.

Odero, Merab, Abigail M. Hatcher, Chenoia Bryant, Maricianah Onono, Patrizia Romito, Elizabeth A. Bukusi, and Janet M. Turan. 2014. Responses to and resources for intimate partner violence: Qualitative findings from women, men, and service providers in rural Kenya. *Journal of Interpersonal Violence* 29 (5): 783–805.

Organization for Economic Co-operation and Development. 2007. "*What is social capital?*" Retrieved 3 Feb 2015 at http://www.oecd.org/insights/379 66934.pdf.

Patterson, Debra, and Rebecca Campbell. 2010. Why rape survivors participate in the criminal justice system. *Journal of Community Psychology* 38 (2): 191–205.

Pease, Bob. 2019. *Facing patriarchy: From a violent gender order to a culture of peace.* London: Zed Books Ltd.

Perry, Steven W. 2022. *Tribal crime data collection activities, 2022.*" *Bureau of Justice Statistics, July.* Washington, D.C.: U.S. Department of Justice.

Price, Joshua M. 2012. *Structural violence: Hidden brutality in the lives of women.* Albany: State University of New York Press.

Przeszlowski, Kimberly, Rob T. Guerette, and Lork K. Sudderth. 2023. The role and impact of the use of information technologies by police in response to violence against women. *International Journal of Environmental Research and Public Health* 20 (6125): 1–18.

Putnam, Robert D. 2000. *Bowling alone: The collapse and revival of American community.* Simon & Schuster: New York, NY.

Ritzer, George, and J. Michael Ryan. 2010. *The concise encyclopedia of sociology.* Hoboken: Wiley.

Rosenblum, Marc R., Irene Gibson, and Sean Leong. 2022. *Fiscal year 2021 southwest border enforcement report: Office of immigration statistics.* Washington: Department of Homeland Security.

Salazar, Mariano, Eliette Valladares, Ann Öhman, and Ulf Högberg. 2012. The supportive process for ending intimate partner violence after pregnancy: The experience of Nicaraguan women. *Violence against Women* 18 (11): 1257–1278.

Samoa Victim Support Group. 2024. *Projects*. Retrieved 16 May 2024 at https://svsg.org.ws/projects-2/.

Sanday, Peggy Reeves. 1981. *Female power and male dominance: On the origins of sexual inequality*. New York: Cambridge University Press.

Schechter, Susan. 1982. *Women and male violence: The visions and struggles of the battered women's movement*. Boston: South End Press.

Sharp-Jeffs, Nicola, Liz Kelly, and Renate Klein. 2018. Long journeys toward freedom: The relationship between coercive control and space for action—Measurement and emerging evidence. *Violence against Women* 24 (2): 163–185.

Sherman, Lawrence. 2018. Policing domestic violence 1967–2017. *Criminology and Public Policy* 17 (2): 453–465.

Smith, Andrea. 2006. Beyond the politics of inclusion: Violence against women of color and human rights. *Meridians* 4 (2): 120–125.

Snider, Laureen. 1998. Towards safer societies: Punishment, masculinities and violence against women. *The British Journal of Criminology* 38 (1): 1–39.

Stark, Evan. 2007. *Coercive control: How men entrap women in personal life*. New York: Oxford UP.

Sudderth, Lori K. 2013. *Services for survivors of sexual assault in St. Lucia*. (Unpublished report for PROSAF, Castries, St. Lucia).

Sudderth, Lori K. 2015. Social networks in safety planning for victims of intimate partner violence: Community, battering, and safety. *Te Awatea Review* 12 (1): 2–5.

Sudderth, Lori K. 2017. Bringing in 'The Ones Who Know Them': Informal community and safety planning for victims of intimate partner violence in New Zealand. *Violence against Women*. 23 (2): 222–242.

Sudderth, Lori K. 2020. Creating safe space in a challenging landscape: Empowerment for rural women in Nicaragua. *International Journal of Crime, Justice, and Social Democracy*. 9 (1): 7–12. https://doi.org/10.5204/ijcjsd.v9i1.1493.

Ullman, Sarah E. 2010. *Talking about sexual assault: Society's response to survivors*. Washington: American Psychological Association.

United Nations. 2003. *The convention on the elimination of all forms of discrimination against women and its optional protocol: Handbook for parliamentarians*. Switzerland: United Nations.

UN Women. 2014. *Services for all women*. New York: United Nations Entity for Gender Equality and the Empowerment of Women. Retrieved 26 March 2014 from www.unwomen.org/en/what-we-do/ending-violence-against-women/services-for-all-women.

Walby, Sylvia. 1990. *Theorizing patriarchy*. Oxford: Blackwell Publishers Inc.

Websdale, Neil. 2001. *Policing the poor: From slave plantation to public housing*. Boston: Northeastern University Press.

Wood, Shannon N., Nancy Glass, and Michele R. Decker. 2021. An integrative review of safety strategies for women experiencing intimate partner violence in low- and middle-income countries. *Trauma, Violence, & Abuse* 22 (1): 68–82.

World Health Organization. 2012. Understanding and addressing violence against women. Retrieved 24 February 2023 at https://apps.who.int/iris/bitstream/handle/10665/77432/WHO_RHR_12.36_eng.pdf.

Yllo, Kersti A., and Murray A. Straus. 1991. Patriarchy and violence against wives: The impact of structural and normative factors. In *Physical violence in American families*, ed. M.A. Straus and R.J. Gelles, 383–399. New Brunswick: Transaction Books.

CHAPTER 2

Rurality, Poverty, Community, and Intimate Partner Violence

Abstract This chapter discusses the challenges of responding to intimate partner violence in rural areas, particularly in low-income countries. Women in low-income countries who survive IPV in rural settings may be hesitant to leave an abusive relationship for several reasons including the proximity of family, traditional gender prescriptions, distance to services, and lack of financial options. Some of these factors are linked to rurality itself, but poverty and adherence to rigid gender expectations exacerbate the challenge of addressing intimate partner violence in these areas. Programming options, including women's empowerment, the inclusion of men, and the use of community to monitor offenders, are discussed.

Keywords Intimate partner violence · Abusive relationships · Rurality · Empowerment · Community · Low-income countries · Survivors/ victims · Gender

In 2007, I spent six months in Costa Rica through the support of a Fulbright traditional scholarship to study their domestic violence policy. The experience was transformative. I had always loved Spanish, and although I could read it, I could not speak the language very well. By

© The Author(s), under exclusive license to Springer Nature Switzerland AG 2024

L. K. Sudderth, *Changing Communities in Challenging Contexts to Address Intimate Partner Violence*, https://doi.org/10.1007/978-3-031-75356-5_2

my fourth month in San Jose, the capital of Costa Rica, I felt comfortable walking into a grocery store, catching a taxi, or stopping someone for directions. I left Costa Rica in January of 2008, and my sense of time had changed, the pace at which I expected to live had slowed, my palate had expanded, and my Spanish was conversational. I also felt a deep love and appreciation for Central America in general—the jungled landscape, the common history of colonial destruction, and the persistence of the women's movement despite a range of challenges from hurricanes and military conflict to gangs and dictatorships. When I interviewed Señora Silvia Mesa, the director of the Women's Institute in Costa Rica, she concluded our chat by saying: "I want little girls to know that they have the right to *expect* that they will live their lives without the threat of violence."

Several years later, I was asked to join the board of the New Haven/León Sister City Project [NHLSCP], a binational non-profit dedicated to *promoting social justice, education and sustainable development in the New Haven and León communities* (New Haven/León Sister City Project 2021). Since I had never been to Nicaragua, in 2016, I joined a NHLSCP women's delegation to Nicaragua. Before the 2018 Mother's Protests that led to the violence and crackdown on nonprofits by the Ortega administration (Hanson and Gomez, 2018), NHLSCP had been regularly sending delegations to Nicaragua since the end of the revolution in the mid-1980s. The delegation I was a part of was small and intimate—four women from the United States with an interest in women's rights in Central America. The delegation was led by a volunteer from NHLSCP, who had been to Nicaragua many times and was fluent in Spanish. The Nicaraguan social worker leading our group on the tour told me something I had heard before: Nico women in violent relationships in rural areas try to find a woman in another village who will take them in and offer shelter until they can figure out their next step.

The Women's Project (El Proyecto de las Mujeres) was a community-based program initiated in 2012 in the village of Goyena intended to address gender inequality and domestic violence, which is extraordinarily high in Nicaragua (Ellsberg, Pena, Herrera, Liljestrand, & Winkvist 1999; U.S. Department of State 2009). These goals were to be achieved through 24 workshops to educate women about their legal rights, the social construction of gender, the dynamics of oppression, preventing intimate partner violence, and to address any victimization through support services. The plan was visionary, and the woman in charge was the perfect super hero for the job: Erendira Vanegas.

Even though she was younger than myself, I could relate to Erendira— we had children around the same age, a boy and a girl, and the resemblance between our offspring was striking. She is very sharp, dynamic, and always upbeat in the meetings with the board. Nevertheless, she is realistic, and adapts to whatever challenges are presented without complaint. She was living under a dictator who later targeted NGOs, especially those associated with the United States; and in 2023, she and her family left Nicaragua for a more stable life in Europe.

The workshops she facilitated in Goyena included discussions of legal options for survivors of gendered violence under (at that time) a new law (Ley 779),[1] which criminalized violence against women. The law was comprehensive and unique in that only two other countries at the time— Spain and Costa Rica—had passed legislation that outlawed violent crimes specifically against women. However, the interpretation of the law and the lack of enforcement weakened the impact considerably. Nevertheless, the women of Goyena were given the opportunity to ask questions of an attorney about their options. They also discussed the social construction of gender, feminism, and other aspects of social justice. The women traveled to Managua as well to take part in International Women's Day celebrations there. I was eager to understand these workshops and their effects.

In Goyena, the American delegation and I sat in on a session of the Women's Project utilizing a Theater of the Oppressed format.[2] The center of this village is an open-air meeting area. There was no hiding who was there or what we were discussing. We were divided into four groups, with each American woman sitting in on a different group. Our task was first to come up with an example of oppression. As a sociologist, I could lecture about oppression all day without notes, but in this company, I was stumped. I talked vaguely about the times that I had realized I was making less money than a man in the same position, whereas, they talked about not having access to water. The only well in the village supplied

---

[1] Ley Integral Contra Violencia Hacia las Mujeres. 2012. Capitulo IIk, pg. 1363. Managua, Nicaragua.

[2] Theatre of the Oppressed is a creation of Augusto Boal, a Brazilian playwright, who uses theatre to educate and transform communities through participatory performances (See Boal, 2020).

water for everyone. There was a pump to get the water, but when the nearby sugarcane company needed water during the dry season, everyone in the village was limited to one bucket of water per family per day. I could not image this. Our next task was to create a human statue that illustrated one example of oppression from the group. We did this improvising with a bottle of water, which I (the oppressor) held in my hand while the others stood in front of me in a pleading stance; one of them held a piece of paper with the word "Agua" written on it. The audience then had to guess what story we were depicting.

Another group had commandeered a small table, and three of them sat around the table with an empty chair. As the story unfolded, the woman sitting to the side revealed her story. She was the oldest in her family, and when her father died, she was told to drop out of school so that her brothers could attend. She wiped away the tears as she pointed out how much she had enjoyed school, and that she wanted to continue (Sudderth 2020). I stood by, listening to her; I had also loved to learn, and I could not imagine being deprived of that prerogative.

In this way, the leader illustrated the connection between oppression and the lives of women in a small village in Nicaragua. The theater exercise had not just instructed, but gave these women the chance to express the impact, to register complaints, to make the link between a gender-based custom, a colonial heritage of industrial power, and their own life chances. Although the project has not been formally evaluated (see Sudderth 2020), informal feedback from the participants suggests layers of effects by an open discussion of oppression—the participants, their children, their partners, and other women in the village, all are impacted, because this is a place where people tend to know each other.

Since my visit in 2016, the Sister City Project has expanded the program to include training women to plant environmentally friendly, individual family gardens. The goal is to empower women by increasing their contribution to the family, lowering food insecurity, and enhancing self-esteem. The training weaves historical perspectives on gender and agriculture with the current underestimation of women's contribution to agriculture worldwide, leading up to practical lessons on preparing the soil for planting. At the end of the project, 15 women from Goyena had planted "kitchen" gardens; they had managed to set up an irrigation schedule and soil conservation plan. A 2023 group photo shows the women and their children proudly holding examples of their work.

RURALITY AND IPV IN THE DEVELOPING CONTEXT

Rurality can be defined by the density of the population, the distance to urban areas, accessibility, the level of privacy, or collective efficacy (e.g., Dax 1996). With the proliferation of suburban populations into rural areas as well as electronic and technological means of communication, the differences between rural and urban populations are less distinct than in the past. Still, rural areas are less densely populated; there is less anonymity, more homogeneity in terms of values, and more densely connected communities (Websdale 1995; DeKeseredy 2021). DeKeseredy and Schwartz (2009) define rural communities by the density of the population rather than by collective efficacy, which varies among rural settings.

The rate of IPV in rural areas of low-income countries ranges from 40 to 67% (Bates et al. 2004; WHO et al. 2013), although any of these percentages may be an underestimate (Leight, Deyessa, and Sharma 2022). In high-income countries, intimate partner violence in rural areas has been linked to patriarchal beliefs, male peer groups that support patriarchal control and abuse of women, higher gun ownership (as well as the fact that rural communities are more accustomed to hearing gunshots from hunting activities), higher pornography consumption, and illegal drug use (see DeKeseredy 2021; DeKeseredy and Schwartz 2009).

In low-income countries, rural women experience gender-based violence in the context of gender expectations that include being responsible for traveling long distances to get water for the family, depending on a husband for financial support, or living with their in-laws (Pommels et al. 2018; Van der Putten and Nur-E-Jannat 2020). The use of violence in a relationship, more rigid gender restrictions, and the difficulty of accessing a sympathetic criminal justice system is often a normative aspect of rural life in low-income countries (Mkandawire-Valhmu et al. 2013; Odero et al. 2014). In rural India, women who work and those who have less decision-making autonomy have increased chances of experiencing abuse (Mogford 2011). Working women are exposed to beliefs and experiences that may lead them to challenge a husband's prerogatives, and in poor families, the wife's work publicly demonstrates the husband's inability to provide for his family; and these factors may lead to abuse (Mogford 2011). In Bangladesh, five or more years of education may provide a buffer for married women in terms of IPV in a way that dowries and registered marriages do not; nevertheless, there is pressure for women to marry young, which typically eliminates chances for higher education (Bates et al. 2004). "In short, the ability of a woman to fulfill her socially defined expectations greatly increases her risk of experiencing violence; men feel justified in acting out physically against their wives if she is perceived to be incapable of providing for the home and family" (Pommels et al. 2018: 1854).

DeKeseredy and Schwartz (2009) provide a model of intimate partner sexual assault in the context of rural women trying to leave or divorce an abusive partner. They link male peer support for patriarchal assumptions about a man's right to control his female partner, and to the threat leaving presents to his masculinity in a context of male proprietariness and societal patriarchy. They link drinking with male friends, particularly those who are abusive themselves and would encourage abuse and patriarchal belief systems. Other factors that are not causal but certainly influential include the use of pornography, illicit drug use, and firearm possession (DeKeseredy and Schwartz 2009). In fact, DeKeseredy and Schwartz (2009) recommend that reducing sexual assault and intimate partner violence in rural areas is possible with a five-pronged approach: (1) raising awareness of IPV in a community through art, PSAs, etc. to change cultural values about violence against women; (2) establishing women's centers in rural areas that not only provide women with safe space to find childcare, information, safety, but also to encourage profeminist connections among rural men; (3) capitalizing on the informal ties in rural areas to increase feelings of safety in public spaces; (4) targeting schools for education about healthy relationships; and (5) developing gender-sensitive environmental designs that reduce crime.

Given the lack of anonymity in rural areas, victims of IPV may worry about stigmatization if they formally disclose their experiences; the pandemic expanded the ability of service agencies to reach out through technology (e.g., zoom) that protects identity but offers tangible contact with a victim advocate or counselor to a wider geographic range of clients (Pedersen et al. 2023). In addition, online training offers service agencies low-cost, efficient ways to provide education about intimate partner violence to a wider rural audience, including police officers, health care providers, social workers, prosecutors, and judges. Social media apps can also offer rural women a place to share their stories with others while maintaining anonymity.

Rurality, then, impacts the experience of intimate partner violence. Some research suggests that, for rural women, connections to family and friends with the day-to-day challenges of transportation, childcare, taking care of the household, etc., act as a buffer to intimate partner violence in a way that they do not for urban women (Lanier and Maume 2009). Those connections "...may serve to compensate for services deficiencies" in rural areas (Lanier and Maume 2009; 1323). "If a woman has contacts to turn to in times of trouble, it is more likely that she will be able to get help. Similarly, increased social support may reduce the 'invisibility' of rural IPV, not necessarily by making private problems more public, but by providing a key source of support in areas with reduced resources and related economic distress at the individual level" (Lanier and Maume 2009: 1323). Collective efficacy, measured by questions about the frequency of socializing with neighbors and the level of confidence that they would help you out in an emergency, seems to suppress crime rates in rural areas, but not intimate partner violence (See DeKeseredy and Schwartz 2009). However, when women did disclose IPV to their neighbors or their religious community, the reaction was stigmatizing for the victim or not helping because of norms around privacy (DeKeseredy and Schwartz 2009). The majority of women in this sample subscribed to patriarchal notions of men being the head of the household, which made it easier for them to set limits on their ability to socialize or connect with others in their community (DeKeseredy and Schwartz 2009).

While rural communities have a depressing effect on public crimes, there is evidence that the close-knit, low anonymity of rural communities does not translate into lower rates of intimate partner violence or sexual violence; even when rural residents witness IPV, they tend not to intervene (Banyard et al. 2019; DeKeseredy and Schwartz 2009). Gallup-Black (2005), in fact, found that in the United States, intimate partner homicides increased significantly in rural areas from 1980 to 1999, even as they decreased in rural and suburban areas. In studies using rural samples in the United States, rural residents describe their communities as generally helpful, but concerns about privacy and how much help the victim wants or "deserves," and the lack of knowledge about what victims of IPV need are all factors in the hesitancy of rural community members helping victims of IPV (Banyard et al. 2019). "Whereas a blind eye referred to potential helpers not wanting to help due to privacy concerns or discomfort with being involved in others' personal lives, many participants indicated that victims keep IPV private, particularly in small towns where everyone knows everyone else's business; thus it may be hard to know it is going on and hard to offer help" (Banyard et al. 2019: 345). Isolation, a normative aspect of abusive relationships, is exacerbated in rural communities because of the lack of transportation and the distance to services (Ceccato 2016; Logan et al. 2005). Therefore, women in rural communities may face unique challenges in leaving an abusive relationship (Ceccato 2016).

Rural women rarely report intimate partner violence to the authorities for many reasons, including the perception that abuse in marriage is normative, the lack of options for safely exiting an abusive relationship in rural communities, and the minimization of the violence (DeKeseredy 2021; DeKeseredy and Schwartz 2009; Secretariat of the Pacific Community 2006). Rural areas often lack the services that would help a victim of intimate violence safely leave the relationship: shelters, social services, employment options, a police force with training in how to respond to IPV, trusted prosecutors ready to pursue conviction, resistance to patriarchal prescriptions for gender, transportation, and community support for divorce (Lewis 2003; Naved & Persson 2005; Sagot 2005; Salazar et al. 2012; Sayem & Khan 2012; Schuler, Bates, & Islam 2008). In rural areas where there are shelters, it is more difficult to keep the location a secret, so abusive men may be a threat to victims in the shelter, as well as the staff who work there (DeKeseredy and Schwartz 2009). In tightly knit communities, police officers and abusive men often know each other, exacerbating the distrust women have in the criminal justice system (e.g., DeKeseredy and Schwartz 2009). Moreover, rural women, compared to urban women, tend to have less education and less understanding of their legal status outside of marriage, which narrows their options (Schuler, Bates, & Islam 2008). Reporting to authorities may, in fact, increase vulnerability for victims who cannot leave their community and cannot trust that the perpetrator will be arrested and prosecuted (Kids in Need of Defense & Human Rights Center Fray Matías de Córdova 2017; Sagot 2005). In addition, the lack of anonymity in rural areas and small towns, where people tend to know each other, suppresses reporting out of fear of stigmatization (DeKeseredy and Schwartz 2009; Logan et al. 2005; Pedersen et al. 2023).

In the study of rural survivors of sexual assault in the context of IPV in Ohio, Dekeseredy and Schwartz (2009) found that the majority of survivors had enlisted the help of a friend, but not anyone near them, "...44 percent sought assistance from the police, and 40 percent received help from a local shelter" (92). Oftentimes, women are isolated by abusers, so they do not have contact with community members enough to reach out for help (DeKeseredy and Schwarz 2009). They also found that law enforcement was often the least helpful of those contacted by survivors, and friends were the most helpful; religious communities tended to be unhelpful, although some survivors clearly appreciated their help. Male abusers tended to have male friends who were also abusive to their partners (Dekeseredy and Schwartz 2009). "In rural sections of Ohio and other states, as we have seen, there is also widespread acceptance of woman abuse, as well as community norms prohibiting survivors from publicly talking about their experiences and from seeking support" (DeKeseredy and Schwartz 2009: 49).

Rural women in low-income countries have few ways of expressing this kind of traumatizing experience. There are no support groups, few shelters, no outlets for leaving an abusive relationship without confronting tradition, and a dearth of resources; moreover, the norms of rural living may include keeping family-related problems within the private sphere (Davies et al. 1998; DeKeseredy and Schwartz 2009; Odero et al. 2014; Sagot 2005). Access to mental health services and a sense of connectedness have been linked to better mental health outcomes in rural areas (e.g., Collins et al. 2017). In small towns in Australia, this sense of connectedness was described as both positive, in terms of the readiness for social support, and negative, in terms of the inevitable chatter of people who know everyone in town (Collins et al. 2017). Few (2005) compared Black and White rural women's experiences in shelters for victims of domestic violence; she found that most of the women were unaware of the shelters in their communities, and while White women reported to the police and found them helpful, Black women more often found support among family and friends, which may have shortened their stays in the shelter. Black women in rural areas worried more about getting assistance from authorities or shelter staff because of concerns about racism, which exacerbated the isolation that is part of abusive relationships; white women were more likely to live near their partner's family, which added to their isolation (Few 2005). Nevertheless, both Black and White women found shelter staff to be supportive and helpful (Few 2005).

Dismantling Intimate Partner Violence

The Women's Project was created to address intimate partner violence in a rural village in Nicaragua, and it was remarkably successful in educating participants about their civil rights, introducing the concept of the social construction of gender, and sparking discussions about interpersonal violence that had been accepted as normative. Given the diversity of rural settings around the world, however, additional programming may be needed to reduce intimate partner violence. There are other examples of programming in rural areas that are reducing IPV around the world, and together with the Women's Project, allows for the framing of some suggestions.

First, many programs reaching out to rural women in developing countries, like the Women's Project, have an educational component, often challenging traditional gender prescriptions, relationship or communication skills, or offering vocational training. Wood, Ludgate, and Mamadnazarova (2021) conducted a small, qualitative study using drawing to get at the perceptions of rural women of empowerment. The participants took part in sex-segregated workshops offered by agricultural extension agents and community health workers in Khatlon Province in Tajikistan. They were asked to listen to the leaders talk about, among other topics, gender-based violence, the impact of violence, and empowerment. The women were given the opportunity to draw two women, one empowered, and the other disempowered, and then discuss the drawing. The exercise suggested that the women saw empowered women as educated, employed, having decision-making power in their household, being liked by others, and being generous with their community (Wood et al. 2021). Challenging traditional gender prescriptions can operate preventively through awareness campaigns aimed at the general public, or specifically targeting women. Banyard et al. (2019) suggested using community norms regarding religion, family, and neighbors to enhance norms around helping victims of IPV. Others recommend workshops focused on supporting victims of IPV, encouraging non-violence in men, or reaching out to faith-based allies (DeKeseredy and Schwartz 2009; Few 2005).

Second, some programs seek to alter the economic dependence of women on men, particularly in rural areas, as a way to either prevent intimate partner violence or as a "path out of an abusive relationship," according Tine Ward[3], CEO and Founder, Rockflower. While intimate partner violence may not be incorporated into the project description, there is evidence that women's financial status can reduce the violence they experience at home. The World Bank provides financing for JEEViKA in India to support the socioeconomic empowerment of women through Self-Help groups that facilitate savings, credit, and loans for rural women's farms, businesses, and training (World Bank 2019).

Rockflower, Inc., for example, is a philanthropic organization that empowers women to become agents of change in their communities (Rockflower, Inc. 2024). Rockflower uses an investment strategy in five key areas: peace and security, maternal and reproductive health, access to food and water, education, and economic empowerment (Rockflower, Inc. 2024). The organization started with small crowdfunding projects for women-led grassroots organizations and female social entrepreneurs. The projects range from educating girls in order to prevent early marriage to factories producing local products (e.g., soap) for sale by women; these are projects that prevent intimate partner violence, because they offer women an alternative to early marriage or to staying in abusive relationships out of financial need (zoom interview, T. Ward, CEO/Founder, Rockflower, 18 April 2024).

Some researchers have recommended vocational training, while others have recommended increasing women's access to land or microfinance loans (Few 2005; Grabe 2010; Kim et al. 2007; Landessa 2024). Gupta et al. (2013) found in a randomized controlled trial in rural Côte d'Ivoire that the combination of village savings and loans association and gender dialogue groups that included male partners reduced intimate partner violence, economic abuse, and justifications for wife abuse. Since tolerance for IPV is positively correlated with support for traditional gender prescriptions (e.g., Bucheli and Rossi 2019), it is important to provide ways to discuss the social construction of gender and its connections to intimate partner violence. Particularly important was the inclusion of male partners in these groups, something that was not always possible in Goyena as many men were employed at a distance. Landessa is an organization that works to secure land rights and land tenure for impoverished men and women around the world. Access to land transforms rural women's status, which positively impacts their health and safety, including

---

[3] I spoke with Ms. Ward through zoom and through email about the philosophy and programming at Rockflower (https://www.rockflower.org). 18 April 2024.

gender-based violence (Grabe 2010; Roberts 2019). Likewise, access to small loans can impact relationships. In South Africa, a microfinance-based intervention that also included education about gender, domestic violence, sexuality, and HIV over a two-year period resulted in the female participants having more confidence in themselves and their financial capacity, as well as more egalitarian attitudes and relationships (Kim et al. 2007). Rural women in low-income countries may also need financial assistance with transportation, childcare, legal advice, housing, and counseling, particularly if they plan to leave the community to escape an abusive relationship (DeKeseredy and Schwartz 2009; Few 2005).

A third idea is to work with women and men on relationship and communication skills, but to bring in other community members to monitor violent spouses. For example, one study in rural Liberia and Sierra Leone, suggested that the main reasons women did not leave their abusive spouses were because of their financial dependence on their husbands and anxiety about what would happen to their children; although most of the women in the study wanted to stay in the relationship, they also wanted the violence to end (Horn et al. 2016). Women's Action Groups (WAGs) facilitated mediation in these relationships, teaching problem-solving and mediation skills, but also helping women to increase their ability to be financially independent (Horn et al. 2016). In addition, Horn et al. (2016) recommended communities take responsibility for holding perpetrators accountable for their actions, incorporating neighbors, chiefs, WAGs, police, and the courts into a collective effort to monitor and change the perpetrator's behavior as well as protect the victim. "The power of a collective, community-level response to IPV emerged strongly from this study, with family members and neighbours as key actors, as well as more formal structures such as WAGs and community leaders" (Horn et al. 2016: 119).

Fourth, like many projects aimed at stopping intimate partner violence, the Women's Project targeted only women for programming, partly because men in the village often worked in other locations, making programming for them more difficult. Studies, in fact, recommend working with men to challenge beliefs about gender, garner support from other men for nonviolent values, and targeting men for educational interventions through health education, discussion about substance abuse, gender, and relationship skills, like empathy and communication skills (DeKeseredy and Schwartz 2009); Jewkes et al. 2002; Mogford 2011; Wood, Ludgate, and Mamadnazarova 2021; World Health Organization

2008). In India, for example, Men's Action for Stopping Violence Against Women (MASVAW), works with men to challenge gender prescriptions that restrict women to narrowly defined roles and underscore male prerogatives to use violence in intimate relationships (Mogford 2011).

Fifth, rural women in the developing world have few places where they can find emotional support or a venue to share their experiences of violence, either with an informed professional or with each other (Carrillo 1993; Sudderth 2020). Instrumental, informal support is negatively associated with intimate partner violence experience in rural areas (Lanier and Maume 2009). If services are available, women in rural areas are less likely to be aware of them, less able to afford them, and more likely to feel that disclosure would bring shame to their families or that intimate violence is normative (Ahrens et al. 2010; Ellsberg et al. 2000; Fanslow & Robinson 2010; Odero et al. 2014). There are two ways that this may be addressed: a) making services in rural areas more visible and more inclusive (Few 2005), and b) increasing remote opportunities to find support through social media, zoom, skype, etc. (Pedersen et al. 2023). Although battered women's shelters are typically not identified as such in order to protect the victims, in small towns and rural areas, it may be difficult to hide that information. Instead, the shelter may be very visible and prominent in the center of town or in a central location. Increased visibility, however, may also expose the victim and staff at the shelter to harassment and abuse (Fagen 2005), but as the director of one such shelter told me, although it threatens the anonymity of the victim, it also exposes the perpetrator to his community. Changing communities, then, to underscore perpetrator accountability enhances safety for the victims.

References

Ahrens, Courtney E., Laura Carolina Rios-Mandel, Libier Isas, and Maria del Carmen Lopez. 2010. Talking about interpersonal violence: Cultural influences on Latinas' identification and disclosure of sexual assault and intimate partner violence. *Psychological Trauma: Theory, Research, Practice, and Policy* 2: 284–295.

Banyard, Victoria L., Katie M. Edwards, Elizabeth A. Moschella, and Katherine M. Seavey. 2019. 'Everybody's really close-knit': Disconnections between helping victims of intimate partner violence and more general helping in rural communities. *Violence against Women* 25 (3): 337–358.

Bates, Lisa M., Sidney Ruth Schuler, Farzana Islam, and Md. Khairul Islam. 2004. Socioeconomic factors and processes associated with domestic violence in rural Bangladesh. *International Family Planning Perspectives* 30(4):190–199.

Boal, Augusto. 2020. *Theatre of the oppressed*, 4th ed. London: Pluto Press.

Bucheli, Marisa, and Maximo Rossi. 2019. Attitudes toward intimate partner violence against women in Latin America and the Caribbean. *SAGE Open* 9 (3): 1–18. https://doi.org/10.1177/2158244019871061.

Carrillo, Roxanna. 1993. Violence against women: An obstacle to development. In *Women's lives and public policy*, ed. M. Turshen and B. Holcomb, 99–113. Westport: Greenwood Press.

Ceccato, Vania A. 2016. *Rural crime and community safety*. Retrieved 5 January 2024. https://doi.org/10.4324/9780203725689.

Collins, Jessica, Bernadette M. Ward, Pamela Snow, Sandra Kippen, and Fiona Judd. 2017. Compositional, contextual, and collective community factors in mental health and well-being in Australian rural communities. *Qualitative Health Research* 27 (5): 677–687.

Davies, Jill, Eleanor Lyon, and D. Monti-Catania. 1998. Safety planning with battered women: Complex lives/difficult choices. Thousand Oaks: Sage Publications.

Dax, Thomas. 1996. Defining rural areas—International comparisons and the OECD indicators. *Rural Society* 6 (3): 3–18.

DeKeseredy, Walter S. 2021. *Woman abuse in rural places*. New York: Routledge.

DeKeseredy, Walter S., and Martin D. Schwartz. 2009. *Dangerous exits: Escaping abusive relationships in rural America*. New Brunswick: Rutgers University Press.

Ellsberg, Mary Carroll, Rodolfo Pena, Andres Herrera, Jerker Liljestrand, and Anna Winkvist. 1999. Wife abuse among women of childbearing age in Nicaragua. *American Journal of Public Health* 89 (2): 241–244.

Ellsberg, Mary Carroll, Rodolfo Pena, Andres Herrerra, Jerker Liljestrand, and Anna Winkvist. 2000. Candies in hell: Women's experiences of violence in Nicaragua. *Social Science & Medicine* 51: 1595–1610.

Fagen, Danielle M. 2005. *Perceptions of collective efficacy among abused women in rural Appalachia*. M.A. thesis, Department of Sociology and Anthropology. Ohio University.

Fanslow, Janet L., and E.M. Robinson. 2010. Help-seeking behaviors and reasons for help seeking reported by a representative sample of women victims of intimate partner violence in New Zealand. *Journal of Interpersonal Violence* 25 (5): 929–951.

Few, April L. 2005. The voices of black and white rural battered women in domestic violence shelters. *Family Relations* 54: 488–500.

Gallup-Black, A. 2005. Twenty years of rural and urban trends in family and intimate partner homicide: Does place matter? *Homicide Studies* 9: 149–173.

Grabe, Shelly. 2010. Promoting gender equality: The role of ideology, power, and control in the link between land ownership and violence in Nicaragua. *Analyses of Social Issues and Public Policy* 10 (1): 146–170. https://doi.org/10.1111/j.1530-2415.2010.01221.x.

Gupta, Jhumka, Kathryn L. Falb, Heidi Lehmann, Denise Kpebo, Ziming Xuan, Mazeda Hossain, Cathy Zimmerman, Charlotte Watts, and Jeannie Annan. 2013. Gender norms and economic empowerment intervention to reduce intimate partner violence against women in rural Côte d'Ivoire: A randomized controlled pilot study. *BMC International Health and Human Rights* 13 (1): 1–12.

Hanson, Lori and Miguel Gomez. 2018. *Deciphering the Nicaraguan student uprising.* NACLA 15 June. Retrieved 18 June 2018

Horn, Rebecca, Eve S. Puffer, Elisabeth Roesch, and Heidi Lehmann. 2016. 'I don't need an eye for an eye': Women's responses to intimate partner violence in Sierra Leone and Liberia. *Global Public Health* 11 (1–2): 108–121.

Jewkes, R., P. Sen, and C. Garcia-Moreno. 2002. Sexual violence. In *World report on violence and health*, ed. E. Krug, L.L. Dahlberg, J.A. Mercy, A.B. Zwi, and R. Lozano. Geneva: World Health Organization.

Kids in Need of Defense [KIND] & Human Rights Center Fray Matías de Córdova. 2017. *Childhood cut short: Sexual and gender-based violence against central American migrant and refugee children.* Available at https://supportkind.org/resources/childhood-cut-short/.

Kim, Julia C., Charlotte H. Watts, James R. Hargreaves, Luceth X. Ndhlovu, Godfrey Phetla, Linda A. Morison, Joanna Busza, John D. H. Porter, and Paul Pronyk. 2007. Understanding the impact of a microfinance-based intervention on women's empowerment and the reduction of intimate partner violence in South Africa. *American Journal of Public Health* 97 (10): 1794–1802.

Landessa. 2024. *What we do: Global Advocacy.* Retrieved 7 May 2024 at https://www.landesa.org/what-we-do/global-advocacy/.

Lanier, Christina, and Michael O. Maume. 2009. Intimate partner violence and social isolation across the rural/urban divide. *Violence Against Women* 15 (11): 1311–1330.

Leight, Jessica, Negussie Deyessa, and Vandana Sharma. 2022. Predictors of discordance and concordance in reporting of intimate partner violence: Evidence from a large sample of rural Ethiopian couples. *Journal of Interpersonal Violence* 37 (23–24): NP23156–NP23179.

Lewis, Susan H. 2003. *Unspoken crimes: Sexual assault in Rural America.* Enola, PA: National Sexual Violence Resource Center.

Ley Integral Contra Violencia Hacia las Mujeres. 2012. Capitulo IIk, pg. 1363. Managua, Nicaragua.

Logan, T.K., Lucy Evans, Erin Stevenson, and Carol E. Jordan. 2005. Barriers to services for rural and urban survivors of rape. *Journal of Interpersonal Violence* 20 (5): 591–616.

Mkandawire-Valhmu, Lucy, Patricia E. Stevens, Peninnah M. Kako, and Anne Dresse. 2013. Safety planning in focus groups of Malawian women living with HIV: Helping each other deal with violence and abuse. *Violence Against Women* 19 (11): 1331–1349.

Mogford, Elizabeth. 2011. When status hurts: Dimensions of women's status and domestic abuse in rural northern India. *Violence Against Women* 17 (7): 835–857.

Naved, Ruchira Tabassum, and Lars Ake Persson. 2005. Factors associated with spousal physical violence against women in Bangladesh. *Studies in Family Planning* 36 (4): 289–300.

New Haven/León Sister City Project. 2021. *Mission and Roots*. Retrieved 18 July 2023 at https://newhavenleon.org/about/mission/.

Odero, Merab, Abigail M. Hatcher, Chenoia Bryant, Maricianah Onono, Patrizia Romito, Elizabeth A. Bukusi, and Janet M. Turan. 2014. Responses to and resources for intimate partner violence: Qualitative findings from women, men, and service providers in rural Kenya. *Journal of Interpersonal Violence* 29 (5): 783–805.

Pedersen, Sarah, Natascha Mueller-Hirth, and Leia Miller. 2023. Supporting victims of domestic violence in rural and island communities during COVID-19: The impact of the pandemic on service providers in north east Scotland and Orkney. *Island Studies Journal* 18 (2): 1–21.

Pommels, Morgan, Corinne Schuster-Wallace, Susan Watt, and Zachariah Mulawa. 2018. Gender violence as a water, sanitation, and hygiene risk: Uncovering violence against women and girls as it pertains to poor WaSH access. *Violence Against Women* 24 (15): 1851–1862.

Roberts, Beth. 2019. Women's land rights: Shifting power for gender equality. Retrieved 21 May 2024 at https://news.trust.org/item/20190531114422-shupv.

Rockflower, Inc. 2024. *Investing in women and girls is the key to global peace and prosperity: Find out how you can help*. Retrieved 18 April 2024 at https://www.rockflower.org.

Sagot, Montserrat. 2005. The critical path of women affected by family violence in Latin America: Case studies from 10 countries. *Violence against Women* 11 (10): 1292–1318. https://doi.org/10.1177/1077801205280189.

Salazar, Mariano, Ulf Högberg, Eliette Valladares, and Ann Öhman. 2012. The supportive process for ending intimate partner violence after pregnancy: The experience of Nicaraguan women. *Violence against Women* 18 (11): 1257–1278. https://doi.org/10.1177/1077801212470549.

Sayam, Amir Mohammad, and Mohammad Aftab Uddin. Khan. 2012. Women's strategic responses to intimate partner violence: A study in a rural community of Bangladesh. *Asian Social Work and Policy Review* 6: 23–39. https://doi.org/10.1111/j.1753-1411.2011.00060.x.

Schuler, Sidney Ruth, Lisa M. Bates, and Farzana Is.am. 2008. Women's rights, domestic violence and recourse seeking in rural Bangladesh. *Violence against Women* 14 (3): 326–345.

Secretariat of the Pacific Community. 2006. *The Samoa family health and safety study*. Retrieved 16 May 2024 at https://pacific.unfpa.org/sites/default/files/pub-pdf/SamoaFamilyHealthandSafetyStudy.pdf.

Sudderth, Lori K. 2020. Creating safe space in a challenging landscape: Empowerment for rural women in Nicaragua. *International Journal for Crime, Justice and Social Democracy* 9 (1): 7–12.

U.S. Department of State. 2009. *2008 Human Rights Report: Nicaragua*. Bureau of Democracy, Human Rights, & Labor. Feb. 25. Retrieved 3/28/13 at http://www.state.gov/j/dr/r/j/hrrpt/2008/wha/119167.htm.

Van der Putten and Amee Nur-E-Jannat. 2020. Coping with domestic violence: Women's voices in Bangladesh. *Journal of Health Research* 36(1):77–88.

Websdale, Neil. 1995. Rural woman abuse: The voices of Kentucky women. *Violence against Women* 1 (4): 309–338.

Wood, Elizabeth A., Nargiza Ludgate, and Camila Mamadnazarova. 2021. Addressing domestic violence as it relates to livelihoods in rural Tajikistan. *Violence against Women* 27 (3–4): 279–294.

World Bank. 2019. "Rural women collectives in India—Translating agency into economic empowerment." Retrieved 6 May 2024 at https://www.worldbank.org/en/results/2019/09/10/rural-women-collectives-in-india-translating-agency-into-economic-empowerment.

World Health Organization [WHO]. 2008. "Preventing violence and reducing its impact: How development agencies can help." Retrieved 10 May 2023 at https://apps.who.int/iris/handle/10665/43876.

World Health Organization, London School of Hygiene and Tropical Medicine, and South African Medical Research Council. 2013. "Global and regional estimates of violence against women: Prevalence and health effects of intimate partner violence and non-partner sexual violence." Retrieved 6 January 2024 at https://www.who.int/reproductivehealth/publications/violence/9789241564625/en/.

CHAPTER 3

Safety and Island Life: Community, Geography, and Intimate Partner Violence

Abstract In this chapter, intimate partner violence disclosure is discussed in the context of living on a small island where people tend to know each other. The chapter begins with a description of some of the challenges of talking about and reporting intimate partner violence in Saint Lucia, a small island in the Caribbean. The literature on intimate partner violence on islands is reviewed along with results from a survey of IPV in Saint Lucia. The chapter ends with a discussion of programming options in the island context.

Keywords Intimate partner violence · Domestic violence · Abuse · Saint Lucia · Islands · Men as allies · Social support · Collaboration · Gender prescriptions · Samoa Victims Support Group · Empowerment

As a brilliant blue sky darkens into a gentle night with a pleasant breeze, I stand on the balcony of my room overlooking Castries Harbour in Saint Lucia. The locusts are buzzing, dogs barking, and traffic signaling commuters anxious to get home. It is soothing to watch the homes nestled into the hills, and their lights like stars in a nearby galaxy. This is home to me, too—a small island of friendly people who never fail to say welcome when I return.

© The Author(s), under exclusive license to Springer Nature Switzerland AG 2024
L. K. Sudderth, *Changing Communities in Challenging Contexts to Address Intimate Partner Violence*,
https://doi.org/10.1007/978-3-031-75356-5_3

I first arrived in Saint Lucia in 2013 at the request of PROSAF (Positive Reactions Over Secrets and Fears), an organization that serves as a resource for survivors of sexual violence on the island. I had met one of their representatives at a professional meeting the previous year, and this had resulted in an invitation to come to the island to conduct a needs assessment of services for sexual assault survivors. A few months later, I happened to sit next to a government official from Saint Lucia at an international conference. I mentioned the request, and he said he knew the organization and the women leading it; he pointed out that they were trying to organize a better response to sexual assault in Saint Lucia, and he hoped I would come and help the cause. It was the first, but not the last time I would encounter the close connections of a small island.

I booked a flight and traveled to St. Lucia in August of 2013. I spent a week interviewing key personnel, including counselors and activists, and I wrote up the report for PROSAF (Sudderth 2013), urging them to include the information in a grant proposal.

In 2015, I received an email from Catherine Sealys[1] of Raise Your Voice St. Lucia, Inc. (RYVSLF), who mentioned that she had read my report. Catherine is the president and founding member of Raise Your Voice St. Lucia, Inc. , an organization created to respond to violence against women with advocacy and resources (Raise Your Voice Saint Lucia, Inc. 2024). RYVSLF, Inc. requested that I do a training for their frontline workers on a collaborative response to sexual assault and intimate partner violence. In January of 2016, I flew back to Saint Lucia, to conduct a two-day workshop, and I have worked as a consultant for RYVSL since that time. It wasn't until my third trip to Saint Lucia, that Catherine said to me as she dropped me off at my hotel, "Wear your shorts tomorrow; we're going around the island." Unlike most Americans who have visited Saint Lucia, I had never been a tourist there; I was intrigued. Catherine gave me an insider's view of Saint Lucia. She stopped at the best places to buy jewelry, arts, and crafts. We visited a caldera, gazed at the Pitons, and marveled at the tropical forest overlooking the

---

[1] I have interviewed and worked with Ms. Sealys on several occasions in the context of my research. As co-founder and president of Raise Your Voice St. Lucia, Inc., she has always given generously of her time and expertise. The interviews cited in this chapter are from a personal interview in June of 2021 and the most recent set of conversations by zoom in May of 2024.

Caribbean Sea. In the middle of the day, we lunched at a small, open-air cafe in the southern part of the island, and even though we were far from Castries in an out-of-way restaurant, Catherine saw someone she knew. I asked her what it was like to live in a place where you routinely run into people you know. She described it as "a double-edged sword." It is comforting to be among familiar faces, she said, but there is also the sense that one is "always being watched." I thought of what I had learned on this island about the challenges of reporting sexual violence in a place where people tend to know each other, the delays in justice once it is reported, and the power of gossip and social media to silence those reports. I had found a research project.

RYVSL, inc. often carried out community assessments in which they asked about experiences of violence, but they did not know what percentage of women in Saint Lucia had experienced intimate partner violence. Dr. Rebecca Hayes had conducted a non-probability survey in Saint Lucia of 102 female participants who answered questions about sexual violence and rape myths. Approximately, one out of every five of the participants had experienced sexual violence in her lifetime (Hayes 2015). Using this research as inspiration, I applied for a Fulbright Scholarship in 2018 to work with RYVSL to conduct a survey on intimate partner violence in Castries, an urban area, and Dennery, a more rural area. I was granted the award—a flex grant allowing two short trips to the island, and I went to Saint Lucia in December 2019 to set up the research. All Fulbright awards were suspended in 2020, so I returned to Saint Lucia in May of 2021 to conduct the survey.

Research on intimate partner violence on islands around the world suggests that 20% to over 60% of women have experienced at least one incident in their lifetime (UN Women 2004; Secretariat of the Pacific Community 2006; World Health Organization 2005). In Samoa, for example, 46.4% of women surveyed had a lifetime experience of some type of intimate partner violence, particularly those women from rural areas, with less education and fewer economic assets (Secretariat of the Pacific Community 2006). In Saint Lucia, we found that 59% of the 241 women surveyed could talk about at least one experience of intimate partner violence in their lifetime, and 25% had experienced IPV in the past year (Sudderth 2022).

ISLANDS AND INTIMATE PARTNER VIOLENCE

For tourists, islands represent an escape to paradise, but for the citizens of island nations, they represent connection and identity (Péron 2004). Cruise ships routinely bring more tourists every year than actually live in Saint Lucia (The Central Statistical Office of Saint Lucia 2023). Islands, like small towns, tend to foster dense networks of people who have known each other for generations. Island life may include relaxed starting times, as well as knowing and being known wherever you go. One early study of criminal victimization on a Caribbean island suggested that, overall, despite feeling relatively safe, island residents experienced higher levels of crime as compared to several high-income countries, but they reported crime to the police less often (Painter and Farrington 1998). The top reason for non-reporting was that the crime was minor, and not worthy of official attention; however, one out of five crime victims knew the offender, and others spoke to the police informally about a crime. Community connections, then, made it unlikely that an official report would be filed (Painter and Farrington 1998).

For women experiencing a violent relationship, those community connections are integral to identity, and in some cases safety; yet they also represent the face of oppression. On the one hand, family and friends on the island offer a sense of home and identity. On the other hand, the disclosure of intimate partner violence or acquaintance rape inevitably involves the possibility of those connections becoming the source of rumor and accusation; in some cases, the family of the abusive partner encourages the violence, reinforcing the gendered hierarchy in traditional heterosexual relationships (Henderson 2017; Hosein 2019; Secretariat of the Pacific Community 2006; Zimmer-Tamakoshi 2012). The violence is derived from and is reinforced by gender norms that give men the authority and women the backdrop for family life (Gibbons 2015). Even the language used by survivors to describe their experiences of intimate partner violence reinforces the hierarchical power of men over women, patriarchal justifications for violence against women, the backlash to women's educational and occupational achievements in the region, and women's resistance to that violence (DeShong 2011, 2015). Certainly, the ravages of capitalism and the struggles of young men to establish masculinity in a changing world have exacerbated violence against women in some contexts (Zimmer-Tamakoshi 2012). DeShong (2015), for example, interviewed 34 men and women from St. Vincent and the Grenadines about gender and their experiences of intimate partner violence. Men talked about violence toward their female partners as justified, based on commonly held assumptions about gender. They rationalized the isolation of their female partner as well as physical violence as a means of upholding her reputation as well as their own. Women interviewees described surveillance, the threat of violence, and the restrictions on their movements, even as they acknowledged the freedom of movement of their male partners. As a result, men had more people in their social network as compared to women and "greater access to social spaces" (92). In the process, traditional conceptions of gender, including the restrictiveness of marriage for women and the normative prerogative of men to police women, were reproduced (DeShong 2015).

In addition, reporting intimate partner violence to local authorities represents the disruption of the underlying current patriarchal norms that frame masculinity and gender prescriptions (Pease 2021; Secretariat of the Pacific Community 2006) as well as the disruption of familial connection. Island networks of family and friends offer a sense of safety, kinship, comfort, and familiarity; but within the context of a violent relationship, "always being watched" makes those connections to extended family and friends challenging to leave. Geography exacerbates the situation, and if a victim fears she will be killed by her partner, escape requires a passport, the resources to leave the country, and start over.

In island societies, victims and/or offenders may know the arresting officer socially, or at least by name, while also expressing skepticism about the efficacy of the criminal justice system (Cleghorn 2023; Painter and Farrington 1998). Moreover, policing responses to intimate partner violence tend to be muted because of the relative absence of law enforcement or because police reports of gender-based violence were more likely related to family feuds or the bias of the responding officer (Lennon 2001; Secretariat of the Pacific Community 2006). If the victim does seek justice in court, routine delays can be deadly (Gaillard 2023; World Bank 2023; phone interview, Sealys, 20 May 2024). The criminal justice system is imported from colonial contexts where anonymity is high and resources, such as funding and space, are more readily available (Maguire and King 2013), although not necessarily victim-centered or trauma-informed.

The challenge to services for IPV victims on islands includes the difficulty of maintaining confidentiality and anonymity (Fairbanks 2022; Pedersen et al. 2023), as well as a justice system that often sides with the abusive male partner (Cleghorn 2023). In addition, an abusive partner (and his allies) may use social media or word-of-mouth to underscore the responsibility of the victim for the abuse or to control her (Woodlock et al. 2023). In St. Lucia, for example, victims are often blamed for an abusive partner's actions, what Catherine calls "anachronistic thinking" (phone interview, Sealys, 20 May 2024).

From my research on intimate partner violence and sexual violence in rural areas, I knew that lack of anonymity had implications for reporting behavior, and that it muddied the rates of intimate violence in rural areas (DeKeseredy 2021; Weisheit, Falcone, and Wells 1994). In addition, sheltering a victim of intimate partner violence on an island is a dance of camouflage, not only because people tend to know one another, but because they tend to talk about what they see. Escape from lethal situations is complicated by geography and limited resources (Sudderth, 2015), because survival may depend on one's ability to leave the country and their connection to family, friends, and jobs. For example, the witness protection system in St. Lucia is handled by one person in an NGO, because the police are not able to maintain a confidential address or to deal with the logistics of hiding someone on a small island.

Islands in the Caribbean share a history of slavery and colonization, which established gender relations, including White male dominance and violence against women (Beckles 2010; Hosein 2019; Randall 2003). Most victims of intimate partner violence do not seek a criminal justice solution, reflecting their skepticism about the efficacy of the system, but also the normative prevalence of this type of violence (Jones et al. 2017; Lazarus-Black 2003; Secretariat of the Pacific Community 2006; Sudderth 2022). In one study of victim interactions with the criminal justice system in Trinidad and Tobago, that skepticism was well placed, as the perpetrator and victim's social status, attributed to the hierarchical ordering of the island's colonial past, influenced access to justice, respect, or empathy; and the lack of transparency in the form of communication and explanation of the justice process left victims feeling anxious, fearful, and alienated (Cleghorn 2023). Similarly, in a study of police reports of sexual violence in Guam, police discretion allowed officers to pursue charges, or not, based on their own personal connection to the case (Lennon 2001). In Saint Lucia, the "interconnection to everyone" is a barrier to disclosure, much less reporting to the police, and victims fear going through the colonial-based court system with its biased judicial appointments and resistance to new domestic violence policies (phone interview, Sealys, 20 May 2024).

More non-western methods of adjudicating gendered violence, such as "custom courts" in some Pacific islands or church mediation may reinforce more conventional paths for married women, including submission to husbands, normalizing male authority in a marriage, failing to recognize non-physical forms of abuse, the lack of support for the mental health needs of victims, or advising victims of violence to marry the abusive man (Bull, George, and Curth-Bibb 2019; Mannell Seyed-Raeisy, Burgess, and Campbell 2018). In Fiji, for example, *bulubulu* is a traditional peacemaking ritual in village life, requiring an apology and a gift from the offender to the victim's family, or more recently, to the victim. Although the ritual was not routinely used for rape or intimate partner violence, the increase in legal penalties for these crimes led to increased use of *bulubulu* as a rationale for reducing punishment (Merry 2006). On the other hand, these community forums do provide public space for discussion of gendered violence and the possibility of publicly holding the offender accountable outside of a criminal justice response (Mannell et al. 2018).

Given these controversies in using traditional methods of resolving conflict, the imposition of more "Western" or international legal responses to intimate partner violence may actually increase reporting and accountability for family violence (see Bull, George, and Curth-Bibb 2019 for review). A prosecutorial response to intimate partner violence may temporarily remove the offender from the community, but it often does little to create support for the victim.

In the capital of Saint Lucia, Castries, women who report intimate partner violence to the police, know that it is difficult to escape the gossip that will follow the report, and often find that the likelihood that the offender will be arrested is the same as a flip of a coin (Sudderth 2022). Participants in our study of intimate partner violence often commented that there was little incentive to report to the police ("Sometimes, based on what you hear other people go through, it makes no sense to go to the police; and they do nothing."—IPV survivor, Castries Central). In one of the workshops I facilitated in Saint Lucia, police officers described the standard protocol for responding to a rape survivor who wanted to report the crime. An officer from the Vulnerable Persons Unit accompanies the victim to the hospital, where they both wait in the waiting room until a

SANE nurse can administer an exam with a rape kit. Sometimes this takes all day, and often the victim knows other people in the waiting room. The police described it as an inefficient use of their time, but it was also clear that this does little to support the victim.

Our research with victims of intimate partner violence echoed these stories. Of the participants who had ever experienced physical violence, sexual violence, controlling behaviors, or emotional abuse, over half disclosed to family (56.1%) or friends (52.0%), and almost a third reported an incident to the police. A little over one-fifth disclosed to a doctor or nurse, often in the context of being treated for injuries. Much smaller percentages of IPV victims spoke to a counselor (18.7%) or clergy (15.0%), and one out of four told no one. Participants in the survey suggested that victims of IPV do not leave their abusive partners, because they are afraid of them, skeptical of the police response, and unsure of what resources would support them:

> "If a lady is abused verbally or otherwise, and they report it, officers will say that's a man/woman thing. I'm not getting involved in that. This should be confidential and investigated. Some women have been killed by their partner. There are known cases where they are abused; it is not reported, but they are victimized at a greater level if they report it. The victim's identity is shared publicly, so they are not comfortable reporting. That has to change" (IPV survivor, Castries South).
>
> "You have to go to the hospital to get a police report, but the system is too long a wait and you end up with no arrest because of no report from a doctor; a better way must be done to help women in order to make an arrest" (IPV survivor, Castries Central).
>
> "Victims don't know better. They don't know where to go....[they need] more education as to where to go" (IPV survivor, Castries South).
>
> "Sometimes victims are afraid; they do not have information as to who to call" (IPV survivor, Dennery South).

SUPPORTING VICTIMS OF INTIMATE PARTNER VIOLENCE

Given the complications of responding to intimate partner violence on an island, NGOs in these countries take on the task of navigating the justice system while working to change the cultural response to violence against women. In a country without paid victim advocates, Raise Your Voice St. Lucia, Inc. volunteers stand by victims of gendered violence as they make their way through the court system, find shelter for victims trying to leave a violent relationship, respond to hotline calls, facilitate workshops and training, continuously apply for funding, lobby for smarter, victim-centered policies, and use research and the media to transform the discussion around gender-based violence. To Catherine, advocacy means, "You have to show up," collaborate with others, attend workshops, work with partners to further the cause, and "do what you say you will do. For an advocate to say nothing is like washing your hands in the dirt." (personal interview, Sealys 2021). Every small island should have a Catherine Sealys to stand up for victims of gendered violence.

Nearby, SAVE Barbados was founded by Liesel Daisley, a survivor of intimate partner violence, with the mission "to help people escape violent and abusive situations—but also to advocate for systemic change" (SAVE Foundation, Inc. 2023). The organization offers a helpline, legal advice, support groups, as well as advocacy for better policies and community education (SAVE Foundation, Inc. 2023).

The COVID-19 pandemic exacerbated the isolation of island life and the difficulty of escaping a violent relationship in that context. Leaving abusive relationships was already arduous, but lockdown rules intensified the complexity of finding safety (Pedersen et al. 2023; Smith-Clapham et al. 2023). On the other hand, the increased use of technology offered unexpected benefits, such as easier training for staff and access to information for the more remote survivors making island life a bit closer to life on the mainland (Pedersen et al. 2023; Péron 2004). The pandemic actually brought alternative methods for reaching survivors on small islands as well as providing training for staff. Pedersen et al. (2023) found in a series of interviews with managers of IPV services in the Orkney Islands that survivors eagerly contributed to an Instagram account that preserved their anonymity and underscored how important it was to hide their identities in this context. Victims of IPV did not want peers to know; they worried about encountering the perpetrator's family and friends, so online conversations were safe (Pedersen et al. 2023). Support, education, and training in island settings can be accessed through technology, such as apps, social media, Zoom, or WhatsApp, assuming a stable connection to the internet. Women living in a violent relationship may not be able to leave children at home to attend meetings or to slip away to another location without being seen, so online options may offer support, awareness education, and access to services.

The Samoa Victim Support Group (SVSG) was founded in 2005 in a vacuum of support for victims in Samoa; the organization has supported 26 initiatives since 2010, including projects targeting men and boys, skills building for youth, economic empowerment of women, and most recently, a research-based project to incorporate indigenous culture into the Samoan response to violence against women (Samoa Victim Support Group 2024a). Their services include shelters, with both schools for children and training for survivors, court support for victims, support for offenders in rehabilitation programs, including anger management, alcohol/drug abuse and offender support groups, counseling and emotional support for victims of intimate violence, hotline support, case management, and prevention work through community involvement; in addition, SVSG offers education and training for the community, including traditional Samoan culture; but the organization also helps communities to take responsibility for addressing intimate partner violence and other types of violence against women (Samoa Victim Support Group 2024b). This strategy includes training community leaders as well as police officers to respond appropriately to intimate partner violence (Samoa Victim Support Group 2024b; UN Women 2023).

CONCLUSIONS

Even though these agencies are social service organizations, they are clearly targeting cultural gender norms that form the backbone of violence against women. It is a delicate approach to a tenaciously difficult web of gender prescriptions, tradition, and the legacy of colonialism (Merry 2006). Appropriate responses to intimate partner violence on an island must take into account the culture and geography of life on the island (Péron 2004). The very definition of family is cultural, subject to colonial imposition; thus broader, local definitions of family may expand and more honestly measure the extent of family violence on an island (Gibbon 2015). First, research on the island context is necessary to establish the extent of intimate partner violence in the population beyond official data and to determine what works in this context. The challenge of changing the response to intimate partner violence on small islands is to not only enhance the criminal justice response, but to recognize the colonial legacy of that system. As such, changing the response to intimate partner violence necessarily involves confronting gender prescriptions that set the stage for abusive relationships.

Second, changing the response to intimate partner violence requires continuous stages of training and education. Multisectoral collaboration brings together law enforcement, health professionals, social workers, and counselors for training on appropriate responses to IPV disclosures. In the island context, this would have to include not only raising awareness about the dynamics of coercive control and intimate partner violence, but underscoring the importance of trauma-informed protocols and confidentiality. Anecdotal evidence suggests that the workshops I facilitated for frontline workers in Saint Lucia were at least temporarily effective. In the two-day workshop, each sector was able to articulate its protocol for responding to IPV, allow other sectors to question that protocol, and then discuss together how to streamline the process with the goal of minimizing the number of times victims share their stories and maximizing the options the victim has at whatever location where they disclose. Fewer complaints from victims were registered in the next several months; rape survivors were ushered into an examining room upon arrival, etc. As is the case in other settings, however, the best-trained workers were promoted, and the complaints mirrored preworkshop levels. This speaks to the need for incorporating this type of exercise into the standard training of employees who work with survivors of gender-based violence, including frontline workers in the medical field, criminal justice, social work, and counseling.

Third, developing educational initiatives that target the community and its leaders for discussions about gender norms and the connections to intimate violence, as well as intervention protocols for individuals and communities is necessary to change the response to IPV. Social media can be used to raise public awareness in primary prevention initiatives, but it can also be used to provide ongoing training for frontline workers, teachers, community and political leaders. Some research suggests incorporating religious leaders into the response to violence against women (Wurtzburg 2003), while others suggest incorporating indigenous cultural beliefs into the formal response to violence against women (Samoa Victim Support Group 2024a, b). Identified communities may provide encouragement, discussion, and/or space for community-based responses to intimate partner violence. In addition, schools can provide students with a curriculum and opportunities to discuss dual-income relationships, the social construction of gender, the changing roles of men and women in marriage, conflict resolution techniques, and signs of abuse (e.g., Gibbons 2015). Educational programming can specifically and purposively help men to become allies to victims of intimate violence, but it can also provide bystander training for men to confront other men about their abusive behavior. In the ideal community, men who work for a construction of masculinity without violence would find support and opportunities for discussion and training (DeKeseredy 2021; DeShong 2015; Gibbons 2015).

Fourth, create opportunities for survivors to discuss their experiences. Even in island nations where support services are available (e.g., SVSG 2024a), there may be cultural constraints on the discussion of gendered violence (The Editorial Board 2022). Nevertheless, it is important to inventory the mental health services available to survivors of intimate partner violence and to maximize their choices for getting the help they need, whether that be legal aid, counseling, childcare, or finding comfort in a support group. Technology may help to orchestrate these efforts, but women who live in low-income areas where there is little systematic support may very well want to meet and talk to each other (Carrillo 1993).

Fifth, interventions based on community must wrestle with the inequality inherited through cultural traditions, religious beliefs, and the imposition of capitalism and colonialism (Zimmer-Tamakoshi 2012). In other words, any response to violence against women must challenge patriarchal norms that keep women financially bound to male partners, reduce women to property, or support male prerogatives to use violence in a relationship. Measures to address structural inequality include community-based interventions to offer women vocational training, education, increased wages, childcare options, and other economic empowerment projects. For victims of intimate partner violence, it means arranging for essential support—housing, sustenance, transportation, court accompaniment, and other initiatives that may require outside support.

References

Beckles, Hilary. 2010. Black masculinity in Caribbean slavery. In *Interrogating Caribbean masculinities: Theoretical and empirical analyses*, ed. R. Reddick, 225–243. Kingston: University of West Indies Press.

Bueno, Cruz Caridad, and Errol A. Henderson. 2017. Bargaining or Backlash? Evidence on intimate partner violence from the Dominican Republic. *Feminist Economics* 23 (4): 90–116.

Bull, Melissa, Nicole George, and Jodie Curth-Bibb. 2019. The virtues of strangers? Policing gender violence in Pacific Island countries. *Policing & Society* 29 (2): 155–170.

Carrillo, Roxanna. 1993. Violence against women: An obstacle to development. In *Women's lives and public policy*, ed. M. Turshen and B. Holcomb, 99–113. Westport: Greenwood Press.

Cleghorn, Leah L. 2023. Victims navigating justice in island communities: An exploration of victims' experiences of the criminal justice system and quality of justice services provided in Trinidad and Tobago. *Island Studies Journal* 18 (1): 52–73.

DeKeseredy, Walter S. 2021. *Woman Abuse in Rural Places*. New York: Routledge.

DeShong, Halimah. 2011. Gender, sexuality and sexual violence: A feminist analysis of Vincentian women's experiences in violent heterosexual relationships. *Journal of Eastern Caribbean Studies* 36 (2): 63–96.

DeShong, Halimah AF. 2015. Policing femininity, affirming masculinity: Relationship violence, control and spatial limitation. *Journal of Gender Studies* 24 (1): 85–103.

Fairbanks, Amanda. 2022. *Zip-tied and left for dead: An Episcopal priest's mysterious end.* New York Times. 6 Feb M1, 6–7.

Gaillard, Sharefil. 2023. *Raise Your Voice confronts surge of domestic violence in St. Lucia.* Loop: St. Lucia News 29 August. Retrieved 24 May 2024 at https://stlucia.loopnews.com/content/raise-your-voice-confronts-surge-domestic-violence-saint-lucia.

Gibbons, Allison Y. 2015. *"Family violence in the Caribbean."* Presentation, expert group meeting on family policy development: Achievements and challenges. United Nations Headquarters, New York. 14–15 May.

Hayes, Rebecca. 2015. *Participatory action research: Identifying and addressing sexual violence in St. Lucia.* Washington, D.C.: Presentation at American Society of Criminology.

Hosein, Gabrielle Jamela. 2019. Masculinism, male marginalization and intimate partner backlash in Trinidad and Tobago. *Caribbean Journal of Criminology* 1 (4): 90–122.

Jones, Adele, Ena Trotman Jemmott, Hazel Da Breo, Tyrone Buckmire, Denise Tannis, Lee Rose, Francia Best, Debra Joseph, and Christian Moller. 2017. *Twenty-one lessons: Preventing domestic violence in the Caribbean.* Retrieved 26 May 2023 at https://www.academia.edu/75894255/Twenty_one_lessons_p reventing_domestic_violence_in_the_Caribbean.

Lazarus-Black, Mindie. 2003. The (heterosexual) regendering of a modern state: Criminalizing and implementing domestic violence law in Trinidad. *Law and Social Inquiry* 28 (4): 979–1008.

Lennon, Daniel A. 2001. Formalizing sexual misconduct on Guam: Family tyrannies and bureaucratic nightmares. *Deviant Behavior* 22 (2): 147–170.

Maguire, Edward R., and William R. King. 2013. Transferring criminal investigation methods from developed to developing nations. *Policing and Society* 23 (3): 346–361.

Mannell, Jenevieve, Iran Seyed-Raeisy, Rochelle Burgess, and Catherine Campbell. 2018. The implications of community responses to intimate partner violence in Rwanda. *PLoS ONE* 13 (5): e0196584. https://doi.org/10.1371/journal.pone.0196584.

Painter, Kate A., and David P. Farrington. 1998. Criminal victimization on a Caribbean Island. *International Review of Victimology* 6: 1–6.

Pease, Bob. 2021. Gendering violence: Theorising the links between men, masculinities and violence. In *Violence, gender and affect: Interpersonal, institutional and ideological practices*, ed. M. Husso, S. Karkulehto, T. Saresma, A. Laitila, J. Eilola, and H. Siltala, 71–90. Cham: Palgrave Macmillan.

Pedersen, Sarah, Natascha Mueller-Hirth, and Leia Miller. 2023. Supporting victims of domestic violence in rural and island communities during COVID-19: The impact of the pandemic on service providers in north east Scotland and Orkney. *Island Studies Journal* 18 (2): 1–21.

Péron, Franoise. 2004. The contemporary lure of the island. *Tijdschrift Voor Economische En Sociale Geografie* 95 (3): 326–339.

Raise Your Voice St. Lucia, Inc. 2024. *Empowering communities, changing lives*. Retrieved 15 May 2024 at https://ryvslu.org.

Randall, Stephen J. 2003. The historical context. In *Understanding the contemporary Caribbean*, ed. Richard S. Hillman and Thomas J. D'Agostino, 51–83. Boston: Lyne Rienner Publishers Inc.

Samoa Victim Support Group. 2024a. "Projects." Retrieved 16 May 2024 at https://svsg.org.ws/projects-2/.

Samoa Victim Support Group. 2024b. "Services." Retrieved 16 May 2024 at https://svsg.org.ws/services/.

SAVE Foundation, Inc. 2023. "About us." Retrieved 15 May 2024 at https://save.bb/about-us/.

Secretariat of the Pacific Community. 2006. *The Samoa family health and safety study*. Retrieved 16 May 2024 at https://pacific.unfpa.org/sites/default/files/pub-pdf/SamoaFamilyHealthandSafetyStudy.pdf.

Smith-Clapham, Amber M., Julia E. Childs, Michele Cooley-Strickland, Joya Hampton-Anderson, Derek M. Novacek, Jennifer V. Pemberton, and Gail

E. Wyatt. 2023. Implications of the COVID-19 pandemic on interpersonal violence within marginalized communities: Toward a new prevention paradigm. *American Journal of Public Health* 113 (S2): S149–S156.

Sudderth, Lori K. 2013. *Services for survivors of sexual assault in St. Lucia.* Castries, St. Lucia: Unpublished report for PROSAF.

Sudderth, Lori K. 2015. Social networks in safety planning for victims of intimate partner violence: Community, battering, and safety. *Te Awatea Review* 12 (1): 2–5.

Sudderth, Lori K. 2022. *Report on experiences and disclosure of IPV in St. Lucia, 2022.* Lucia Inc: Unpublished Fulbright-funded report for Raise Your Voice St.

The Central Statistical Office of Saint Lucia. 2023. *Tourist arrivals by country of residence, 2018 to 2023.* Retrieved 16 May 2024 at https://stats.gov.lc.

The Editorial Board. 2022. *A culture of violence and abuse. Samoa Observer,* 26 November. Retrieved 17 May 2024 at https://www.samoaobserver.ws/category/editorial/100740.

UN Women. 2023. *Global database on violence against women.* Retrieved 1 June 2023 at https://evaw-global-database.unwomen.org/en/countries/oceania/samoa.

Weisheit, R.A., D.N. Falcone, and L.E. Wells. 1994. *Rural crime and rural policing.* Washington, DC: U.S. Department of Justice.Pe.

Woodlock, Delanie, Michael Salter, Molly Dragiewicz, and Bridget Harris. 2023. 'Living in darkness': Technology-facilitated coercive control, disenfranchised grief, and institutional betrayal. *Violence against Women* 29 (5): 987–1004.

World Bank. 2023. *Gender-based violence country profile: Saint Lucia.* Retrieved 24 May 2024 at https://doi.org/10.1596/40135.

Wurtzburg, S.J. 2003. The Pacific Island community in New Zealand: Domestic violence and access to justice. *Criminal Justice Policy Review* 14 (3): 423–446.

Zimmer-Tamakoshi, Laura. 2012. Troubled masculinities and gender violence in Melanisia. In *Engendering violence in Papua New Guinea,* ed. M. Jolly, C. Stewart, and C. Brewer, 73–105. Canberra: Australia National University E Press.

CHAPTER 4

Tribal Communities, Safe Space, and Intimate Partner Violence

Abstract This chapter considers the challenges of responding to intimate partner violence in tribal communities, where kinship ties are key to mental health and identity. The historical context of colonization, genocide, and the imposition of patriarchal values on family life is the backdrop for understanding intimate partner violence among indigenous women, the limitations of informal support, and the failures of the criminal justice response. Recommendations include the incorporation of indigenous values into the response to intimate partner violence, using community-based advocacy to hold the offender accountable and keep indigenous women safe.

Keywords Intimate partner violence · Indigenous · Tribal · Colonization · Informal networks · Disclosure · Restorative justice · Peacemaking · Coordinated community response

In 2014, I received an email introduction from a social work professor at the University of Canterbury in Christchurch, New Zealand. The introduction came with an invitation to consider a faculty exchange—she wanted to do some research in the United States and needed a base of operation. In exchange, I could spend a few months in New Zealand with

© The Author(s), under exclusive license to Springer Nature
Switzerland AG 2024
L. K. Sudderth, *Changing Communities in Challenging Contexts to
Address Intimate Partner Violence*,
https://doi.org/10.1007/978-3-031-75356-5_4

the use of her office and the resources available through her university. I had no idea what type of research I could do in New Zealand, but the opportunity was undeniably intriguing, so I agreed.

Dr. Annabel Taylor came to the United States in the fall of 2013, and she occupied an office just down the hall from me. We had lunch together quite often, and our discussions were among the most stimulating and inspiring conversations I have had with a colleague. Dr. Taylor shared my interest in policies and practices addressing violence against women, and she was familiar with the history and culture of the Indigenous people of New Zealand, the Maori. The social service model in New Zealand was not only to provide professional intervention in intimate partner violence, but to encourage informal supports to intervene as well (Crichton-Hill and Taylor 2013; Ministry of Social Development 2009). I learned that this model was sensitive to the needs of Maori cultural values and incorporated Maori families (whanau) into the response to intimate partner violence. We talked about the similarities in the effects of colonization and genocidal policies on the tribal communities in the United States and New Zealand. Our discussions inspired my curiosity about the role of a tribal community and victim advocacy in response to victimization.

In 2014, I spent three glorious months interviewing 24 victim advocates at battered women's refuges in New Zealand. I took a class in the Maori language at a local high school, and I connected with the teacher in conversations about Maori history and my own limited knowledge of my Native American ancestors. I learned that incorporating Maori values into the social service response to intimate partner violence meant including a social network of people who would monitor the victim and keep her safe, whether or not she sought residence in a temporary shelter. It meant addressing victimization *and* preserving community connections, educating victims *and* family members about the dynamics of intimate violence. Even though my time in Aotearoa (the Indigenous name for New Zealand) was relatively short, I felt like I had a new understanding of community-based advocacy.

INDIGENEITY AND VICTIM ADVOCACY

Indigenous peoples is a phrase that captures the diversity of the indigenous people around the world; it indicates that "indigenous" refers not to one group, but to diverse groups. Indigenous peoples have unique cultures and histories but may include colonization, assimilation experiences meant to erase cultural identity, struggling with the sovereignty of non-indigenous governments, the dissolution of tribal connections through individual oppressive policies, the loss of territory as well as a unique and inseparable connection to the areas linked to their ancestors (Holt 2001; Mann 2022; McNeish and Eversole 2005). However, tribal cultures vary significantly in terms of gender prescriptions and intimate partner violence (Hamby 2000), which underscores the importance of addressing intimate partner violence on the community level.

INDIGENOUS WOMEN AND IPV

Historically, Indigenous women in the Americas experienced less intimate violence than their European counterparts, because women were leaders, teachers, farmers, the keepers of culture, and violence against women was not sanctioned by most tribes (Agtuca 2008; Baskin 2020). For many Indigenous peoples, rape is a crime against the community as much as it is against the person (Deer 2015). European colonization marginalized Indigenous women legally and socially, imposing a patriarchal, racially biased framework on what had been a more balanced, communal life (Baskin 2020). Although treaties with the United States recognized tribal authority over the criminal behavior of its citizens, the sovereignty of Indian nations was gradually watered down through legislation and judicial decisions (Agtuca 2008).

While there are no international statistics on intimate violence against Indigenous women, country-specific studies consistently indicate that Indigenous women experience higher rates of intimate partner violence than non-Indigenous women (e.g., Bachman 2008; Rosay 2016). In North America, Indigenous women have higher rates of intimate partner violence as compared to non-Indigenous women (Bachman et al. 2008; Heidinger 2021; Perry 2022; Rosay 2016). For example, Statistics Canada reports that 62.7% of Indigenous women had experienced physical or sexual assault by an intimate partner, as compared to 44.7% of non-Indigenous women (Heidinger 2021). The U.S. Bureau of Justice Statistics reports on offenders held in Indian County jails, and in 2020, 17% of inmates were there because of domestic violence (Perry 2022).

The higher rates of intimate partner violence among Indigenous populations are attributed to colonization, racism, patriarchy, poverty, rurality, high unemployment, and the lack of inherent authority given to tribal governments to deal with crime, rather than to traditional cultural values (Agtuca 2008; Baskin 2020; Burnette 2016; Hamby 2000; Odera et al. 2014; Oetzal and Duran 2004; Rose 2012; Smith 2005; Ybanez 2008). In low-income countries, intimate partner violence against Indigenous women is associated with gender prescriptions, being unaware of women's rights or the social services that support survivors of intimate partner violence, male use of alcohol, and maternal health (Wands and Mirzoev 2022). Individual-level risk factors for intimate partner violence in Indigenous populations include being female, 16–24 years old, unemployed, lower educational level, lower income/welfare, and using alcohol, but a protective factor is a cultural connection to the tribal community (See Oeztal and Duran 2004 for review). Gender prescriptions and family bonds influence risk on the interpersonal level, and on the organizational level, the lack of routine screening for intimate partner violence in health settings and the lack of services set up to address intimate partner violence both increase the risk for victimization (Oetzal and Duran 2004).

On the community level, colonization increases the risk of intimate partner violence in Indigenous communities, because it historically disrupted and destroyed Indigenous cultures, including tribal responses to crime, the ways men and women related to each other, and traditional ways that men earned status, traumatizing subsequent generations (Brave Heart and DeBruyn 1998; Clairmont 2008; Coker 2006; Duran et al. 1998; Oeztal and Duran 2004; Weaver 2009). Around the world, Indigenous communities have struggled with sovereignty and self-determination in efforts to fight poverty and improve the well-being of its members (e.g., Humpage 2005). Traditionally, while gender arrangements varied in tribal communities, the role of women ranged from farmers to familial and cultural leaders, sharing stewardship of the land. European law framed men as farmers and individual men as owners of the land, and in imposing their own system on Indigenous people, took economic power away from women (Agtuca 2008). After colonization, Indian nations were no longer able to police their own citizens, rather, they were subject to policing by the government that colonized them.

Colonization, which introduced stricter gender prescriptions to Indigenous cultures, exacerbated violence against women (Oetzel and Duran 2004). Moreover, the imposition of nuclear family arrangements, as well as Christianity, on Indigenous cultures increased intimate partner violence while subjecting victims to a criminal justice system that reinforces patriarchal assumptions (Arnull and Stewart 2021; Jolly 2012;

Merry 2006; Zorn 2012). Consequently, Indigenous survivors of intimate partner violence may not feel comfortable turning to that same oppressive power for assistance. Victims, in fact, may be more trusting of their own informal networks rather than local law enforcement; at the same time, the cultural pressure to maintain family connections may discourage disclosure altogether (see Willis 2011).

Disclosure of intimate violence, in fact, is complicated by connections to the tribal community, as well as fear of a perpetrator who is enmeshed in that same community (Meyer and Stambe 2021). Indigenous survivors hesitate to report sexual violence or intimate partner violence to authorities, because they fear the ostracizing reactions of family and community or the criminal justice system itself (Amnesty International 2007; Clairmont and Deer 2008; LaPointe 2008; Taylor and Mouzos 2006; Taylor and Putt 2007; Willis 2011). Wild and Anderson (2007) found that when Indigenous survivors anticipate "inadequate or culturally inappropriate" reactions, they are less likely to report the crime to authorities. They may also fear the perpetrator or the possibility of further violence, and struggle with the normalization of violence that may be considered a "private" or a "family" matter (Amnesty International 2007; Begay 2020; Clairmont and Deer 2008; Mullighan 2008; Taylor and Mouzos 2006; Taylor and Putt 2007; Willis 2011). Donovan et al. (2010) found that Indigenous survivors of sexual violence were slightly more likely than non-Indigenous survivors to be worried about upsetting their parents. Even tribal members who want to intervene in a violent relationship may be concerned about the community response to their actions in addition to possible retaliation by the offender (Taylor and Mouzos 2006).

This pattern repeats itself in Indigenous communities around the world. Non-disclosure of intimate violence is related to minimizing the seriousness of the crime, negative perceptions of how the criminal justice system will respond, beliefs in myths about intimate violence or gender, and fear of how others would react (e.g., Gurm and Marchbank 2020; Krug et al. 2002; Weaver 2009). In addition, the U.S. government-imposed limits on the prosecution of violence against Native American women which means that intimate partner violence, sexual violence, stalking, and other forms of violence against women are less likely to come to the attention of authorities and less likely to be penalized if they are reported (Gilbert et al. 2021).

Hill (2008), in fact, makes the point that the coercive and controlling tactics of batterers mirror the tactics of colonization. In these contexts, escape from an abusive relationship is more difficult, because of the dearth of resources—e.g., affordable housing, transportation—the distrust of the criminal justice system, and the lack of confidentiality (Amnesty International 2007; Bosch and Schumm 2004; Burnette 2015a, b; Jones 2008; Wands and Mirzoev 2022). But, Indigenous women living outside the tribal context may also find it challenging to leave their extended family for an urban refuge that may not be aware of the impact of colonization over the generations, and thus, insensitive to the needs of Native women (Clark and Johnson 2008).

Because of concerns about confidentiality and community reaction, Indigenous survivors may be more likely to rely on informal networks of support rather than reporting to authorities (Gauthier et al. 2021; Meyer and Stambe 2021; Willis 2010). Native women may also be more likely to turn to informal sources of support because of cultural norms for dealing with trauma (Burrage et al. 2021; Shepherd 2001) and the difficulty of accessing services in rural areas, for those living on reservations (See Burrage et al. 2021). Australian Indigenous survivors were more likely to turn to informal networks and the medical community rather than to the police (Willis 2010). Moreover, there is a legacy of distrust of authorities, given the historical context in which colonizing governments controlled the legal penalties against perpetrators who abused Indigenous women, and the continued inadequacy of the criminal justice response to these crimes (Amnesty International 2007; Willis 2011). Gauthier et al. (2021), however, suggest a more nuanced approach to help-seeking among Indigenous populations, in that they suggest, the more integrated Indigenous women are into a community, the more they rely on an informal (rather than formal) support system. For example, they asked a sample of Indigenous women if they would refer a domestic violence victim to informal or formal support systems or to no one at all. Women who were connected to a community through cultural traditions, housing assistance, or a recovery support group were more likely than more isolated or disadvantaged women to recommend informal support. Given the rural context of many Indigenous communities, the preference for informal supports is not surprising; but it also speaks to the distrust of more formal mechanisms for addressing intimate partner violence.

Colonization and the failure of law enforcement agencies to intervene in intimate partner violence have led to distrust of the criminal justice response (Mullighan 2008; Wild and Anderson 2007; Smith 2005; Willis 2011). The criminal justice system has disproportionately targeted tribal communities, including women of color who have survived gendered violence, for incarceration; therefore, women in tribal communities place less trust in the criminal justice system to address intimate partner violence (Smith 2005). Smith (2005) writes about the intersection between violence based on patriarchy and violence based on colonialism: sexual violence is intertwined with the subjugation of Native American culture. While the battered women's movement successfully advocated for a criminal justice response to domestic violence, Smith (2005) argues that women of color cannot find refuge in a system that has been responsible for the abuse of marginalized communities. On reservations and in rural areas, the response of law enforcement is often delayed by distance, leaving battered women who call the police vulnerable to more abuse (Ned-Sunnboy 2008). Women also do not report because of lack of services, or they are not aware of the services available, language barriers, lack of transportation from remote areas, or the absence of trained police officers who could effectively and sensitively respond to Indigenous victimization (Willis 2011). However, in low-income countries, the poverty of Indigenous communities, as well as the normalization of IPV, limits the help that informal contacts can offer to women trying to escape an abusive relationship (Wands and Mirzoev 2022).

Policies Addressing Intimate Partner Violence in Indigenous Communities

Pre-colonization tribal laws held men accountable for the abuse of women (Baskin 2020). Particularly in matriarchal cultures, violence against women would have violated sacred beliefs about relationships and the balance of life; violence against women, the idea of valuing males over females in a hierarchical social structure, and internalized racist and sexist beliefs all came from colonization (Hill 2008).

In North America, tribal communities traditionally used community-focused approaches to respond to criminal behavior, including the use of well-respected warriors to provide protection for the community when needed, responding to infractions of community standards that were reported by community members, and holding offenders accountable through mediation that led to reparations, shunning, banishment (Twiss 2008). Community members guided the offender, and the community monitored him, but it was his responsibility to change his behavior (Twiss

2008). In a 2022 article for *National Geographic*, Quanah Rose Chasinghorse pointed out, "Our voices, experiences, stories, cultures, and traditions aren't recognized the way they should be. We carry so much knowledge, strength, and power, not just trauma and pain." (Yüyan 2022: 136). Twiss (2008) advocates a probation model that incorporates some of these ideas, that is, the integration of traditional tribal practices into the criminal justice response to domestic violence offenders. In other words, tribal probation officers should incorporate "…coercive power of the community to shape and change criminal behavior" (Twiss 2008: 313). This would include multiple agencies, the offender's family, the victim, the victim's family, and other members of the community to develop an individualized plan for change, prioritizing the safety of the victim (American Probation and Parole Association 2009; Twiss 2008). The plan would include accountability, not only to the probation officer, but to the community, with clear consequences for violation of the terms of the agreement (Twiss 2008).

Policies addressing intimate violence in tribal communities must address both the impact of colonialism and the impact of gendered violence, but often policies only address one or the other (Smith 2012). Punitive-based policies that include incarceration are products of the same system that decimated Native American populations in the nineteenth century and maintains oppressive conditions today; however, for tribal survivors of intimate partner violence and sexual assault, there are few options but to entrust the prosecution to that system (Smith 2012). Supportive national policies may be limited in their effects on Indigenous communities, because few government plans to prevent domestic violence in the Global North include Indigenous perspectives or discuss structural racism or the impact of colonization (Fotheringham, Wells, and Goulet 2021). In the United States, for example, historically the policies of the U.S. government limited the prosecution of violent crimes committed against Native American women, first through the Major Crimes Act of 1885, which placed the prerogative of prosecution of certain violent crimes against Native Americans in the hands of the Federal government (18 USC 1153), one of many actions eroding tribal authority in the nineteenth century (Agtuca 2008). Public Law 83–280 authorized state enforcement of laws on reservations in some states, and this continues to cripple law enforcement on reservations (Agtuca 2008). Colonization stripped tribal control over the prosecution of crimes against their own people, replaced non-hierarchal, gender-fluid governing structures with rigid patriarchal beliefs, and denigrated Native American status (Deer 2015; Luna-Gordinier 2018; Weaver 2009).

The Indian Civil Rights Act of 1968, which was supposed to bring Constitutional rights to Native American tribes, actually lowered penalties for crime against Native American women, because tribal authorities could not sentence an offender to more than one year of incarceration, a $5,000 fine or both, for sexual assault or domestic violence convictions (Deer 2015). Moreover, the Supreme Court ruled in *Oliphant v. Suquamish* (1978) that tribal courts were restricted in holding non-Native offenders accountable for crimes against Natives. All of these changes resulted in few consequences for violence against Native women, since the majority of sexual assaults are committed by non-Native men (Begay and Zandamela 2018; Tjaden and Thoennes 2000).

The Violence Against Women Act [VAWA] of 2022 changed the direction of 300 years of policy toward Native Americans by providing funding for efforts to combat violence against women and granting tribal governments the authority to criminally prosecute non-Native perpetrators of intimate partner violence in Indian territory. Even as the response to intimate partner violence has improved in many countries (Weldon 2002), it is not clear how these policies serve Indigenous survivors, because translating national policy to the local context is dependent on understanding the community level of intimate partner violence and the local response to it (Merry 2006). Ned-Sunnyboy (2008) articulates the problem of the "helicopter justice" approach to intimate violence. In Alaska, Native survivors of intimate partner violence are sent to shelters in cities, far from their support system; male perpetrators from Alaska tribal communities are mandated to treatment programs developed for non-Indigenous men, resulting in a high failure rate. In small communities where the rate of intimate partner violence is high, one arrest can trigger conflict between entire families, and it can lead to further, retaliatory violence (Ned-Sunnyboy 2008). Moreover, Indigenous women leave behind connections to land and extended family; they face formidable financial and emotional challenges in exiting the tribal community (Ferraro 2006). Ybanez (2008) points out that shelters have seldom been built in Indigenous communities because of the lack of funding, the lack of confidentiality, and the rural context of reservations, which makes protection from a law enforcement agency difficult. Police, in fact, do not always offer support to victims in Indian country (Ybanez 2008). Moreover, the system from which Native women seek help is the same one that once removed Native children from their families to place them in boarding schools, the system that fails to investigate the disappearance of Native women, and the system that incarcerates Native men with longer, federal sentences. "Often we find that we are adopting mainstream models that are authoritative and paternalistic. These punitive models serve to reinforce battered women as defective and fail to honor individual women for who they are" (Ybanez 2008: 61). The challenge for practitioners and policymakers is to restore community power for healing, accountability, and preventing intimate partner violence, as well as other types of gender-based violence (Smith 2005, 2012).

Native women in the US may move to urban areas to find work or to take advantage of other resources available in cities, including health care, shelters, and transportation, but family, friends, and culture are left behind. That loss is intensified for Indigenous women who lean on their informal support to cope with structural oppression (Price 2012; Renzetti 1992). This leaves them feeling isolated; it exacerbates the difficulty of sheltering far away from extended family and tribal connections (Clark and Johnson 2008). They may be hesitant to report IPV, because they are unaware of the services available to them, they fear losing custody of their children, and there are few services catering specifically to Native women (Clark and Johnson 2008).

For those survivors on reservations, tribal courts and law enforcement may be limited by corrupt, informal connections between the perpetrators of intimate partner violence and criminal justice personnel, the lack of training in recognizing intimate partner violence, and the inability of the tribe to enforce protective orders or hold offenders accountable (Hill 2008; Ned-Sunnyboy 2008). As in other rural areas, when the perpetrator knows, or is related to a leader in the community, law enforcement, or the courts, the enforcement of the protection order is often nullified. In remote areas of Alaska, tribal communities have the authority to ban a perpetrator from the community, but this requires a multidisciplinary approach to enforcing such a penalty (Ned-Sunnyboy 2008).

Recommendations

The UN Committee on the Elimination of Discrimination Against Women (CEDAW) recommends that countries "Adopt and effectively implement legislation that prevents, prohibits, and responds to gender-based violence against Indigenous Women and Girls incorporating a gender, Indigenous Women and Girls, intersectional, intercultural, and multidisciplinary perspective..." (UN Women 2022). But, national policies have to be translated into local, community-based solutions that include incorporating local cultural practices into the response in cooperation with community members (Merry 2006). The following are recommendations for community-based programming to address intimate partner violence in tribal communities.

1. Training for tribal leaders and criminal justice personnel. Given the structural as well as the individual barriers to reporting intimate partner violence to authorities, the first recommendation would be strategically and continuously provide training and educational programming. The training should include cultural sensitivity and civil rights, in addition to the risk factors for intimate partner violence. The programming should target any points in the criminal justice, medical, mental health, or judicial systems where Indigenous communities would report intimate violence. This includes healthcare professionals, social workers, religious leaders, and community leaders, as well as police officers and criminal justice personnel to underscore the appropriate response to disclosure and the importance of confidentiality (Oetzel and Duran 2004; Willis 2011). Educational workshops that target potential, current, or past victims of intimate partner violence should include safety planning and risk factors for intimate violence, but also the role of colonization in the violence perpetrated against them (Ybanez 2008).

2. Build infrastructure that includes economic empowerment of women. Many of the organizations that support the empowerment of women include the reduction or elimination of violence against women in their objectives, even if they differ in how they accomplish this. Oxfam (2023) empowers Indigenous women by supporting their decision-making powers in access to tribal land. Rural Indigenous women, in particular, may need assistance in bringing legal cases of abuse before the courts in order to increase the likelihood that offenders are held accountable (Amnesty International 2007; Women's Justice Initiative 2022). The Women's Justice Initiative (WJI) is a non-profit organization based in Guatemala that addresses violence against rural, Indigenous women and girls through "community-based solutions" in local indigenous languages (Women's Justice Initiative 2022). WJI provides free legal

advice on cases involving violence against women; they work with government and community agencies, including police and community leaders, to strengthen the response to intimate violence; they offer legal and empowerment education (Women's Rights Education Program), as well as community leadership training for women; subsequently, the trained advocates mentor girls in the Adolescent Girls Program, teaching them about their civil rights and delaying marriage (Women's Justice Initiative 2022).

3. Incorporate tribal healing practices into personal therapeutic programming for survivors and perpetrators of intimate partner violence. Indigenous communities may suffer from intergenerational trauma similar to the descendants of Holocaust survivors, and thus may benefit from traditional ceremonies acknowledging grief (Brave Heart and DeBruyn 1998). Therapeutic and supportive programming for Indigenous survivors of intimate partner violence is most effective when cultural and/or artistic practices of tribal communities are incorporated into the intervention (Giesbrecht et al. 2022; Jones 2024; Oden and Balog-Patrick 2024). Oetzel and Duran (2004) recommend in addition to therapeutic approaches that incorporate traditional healing practices, home visits for Native American survivors of intimate partner violence because they were less likely to have transportation to a domestic violence program, but also to increase trust. They suggested, for example, based on other research (e.g., Durst 1991), that when tribal leaders speak to a couple in conflict, and historical trauma is addressed using traditional healing rituals, there was a greater impact on the larger community in terms of attitudes and interventions. Indigenous women with experience as survivors of intimate partner violence may be especially qualified to encourage survivors to be comfortable, safely share their stories, and cultivate resilience in other Indigenous survivors (Holder 2023; Willis 2011).

In Indigenous communities, the key to addressing intimate partner violence is to restore community powers of healing, and to incorporate the community into the healing process and the prevention process (Ned-Sunnyboy 2008). That means reconceptualizing the crime of intimate partner violence as a crime against a community, rather than as an individual crime. It also means re-introducing traditional beliefs about community and the ownership of problems and solutions (Ned-Sunnyboy

2008). For example, the Maori concept of family includes extended family—cousins, aunts and uncles, sisters and brothers of grandparents, etc., and traditionally, a crime against one person was a crime against the whole family. Therefore, in New Zealand, out of sensitivity to Maori customs, victim advocates first ask a victim of intimate partner violence about their social support and their *whanua* [family] (see Sudderth 2017). Who can come with you to the meeting? Who is your *whanua*? Restorative justice practice, based on traditional Maori methods for dealing with crime, involves a meeting between the two families. Similarly, in safety conferencing, victim advocates meet with the family and friends of the victim, so that the social support of the victim becomes part of her safety plan (Pennell and Francis 2005; Mirsky 2003). This option may be preferable to Native women who cannot or will not leave their community for a shelter.

4. Address the historical/generational trauma in Indigenous communities by acknowledging the effects of colonization and genocide in addition to intimate partner violence. The struggle of Indigenous women to create a safe space is intertwined with tribal claims of territory that was colonized by non-Indigenous governments. Some tribes have begun to reclaim their land, while others work for the acknowledgment that Indigenous people lived on the land before European settlement (Keomoungkhoun 2020). The Tla-o-qui-aht in British Columbia, for example, are working to undo the damage of colonial logging companies in their traditional homeland, including control of educational programming, hiring of park rangers, and lobbying businesses to take some financial responsibility for conservation work (Mann 2022). Part of what is being restored is a sense of community, rather than a continuation of individual greed and profit; this is community empowerment as much as a protest against colonization and genocide. Hamby (2000) points out that each tribal community is different in terms of gender relations, so one cannot generalize other than to say all tribes have been subjected to colonization. Based on this, Hamby (2000) recommends taking into account the unique cultural constructions of gender and approaches to intimate partner violence as part of the intervention in intimate partner violence; communities are resources, and should be part of the solution as opposed to taking interventions from Western communities and applying them to

Indigenous communities. Hamby (2000) points out that the combination of colonization, racism, and lower socioeconomic status increases the risk of intimate violence among American Indians.

In addition, a coordinated multidisciplinary team approach to intimate partner violence in tribal communities with wraparound services is needed to meet the needs of Indigenous survivors (Meyer and Stambe 2021; Oetzel and Duran 2004) as well as community healing rituals, opportunities for communities to discuss how to respond to intimate violence, resources to do this, and an increase in employment opportunities. Some tribal communities may be interested in a restorative justice approach to intimate partner violence, more than non-tribal communities, because it is consistent with tribal practices to control crime (Nancarrow 2016).

Hill (2008) recommends a coordinated community response to violence against Indigenous women, led by victim advocates, but including law enforcement, court representatives, and providers in men's programs. Women's safety and batterer accountability are possible through communication, education, and sound policy decisions that are sensitive to the cultural background of tribal communities (Clairmont and Deer 2008; Hill 2008).

The role of advocacy is to respond to the individual crisis, but to also work to change the social, economic, institutional, and political conditions that precipitate the crisis (Hill 2008; Meyer and Stambe 2021). There are two models of advocacy: one is a social service model that is focused solely on the needs of the individual victim. This type of advocacy is necessary, but it does not challenge the social structure; in fact, it helps individual victims to adapt to the constraints of the social structure (Hill 2008). The social change model, however, is focused on the intersection of individual experience and oppressive, historical, and political structures that set the stage for violence (Hill 2008: 198). This model, then, is focused on changing the structure that encourages the victimization in the first place, and it requires the safety of women and respectful treatment of victims of intimate violence (Hill 2008). For Indigenous communities that have suffered from the effects of colonization and genocide, the latter model is a better fit.

5. Integrate tribal practices into the formal response to intimate partner violence. Given the need to enhance tribal authority and address

racial discrimination in the criminal justice system (Amnesty International 2007), the final recommendation is to use the strengths of tribal culture to address intimate partner violence. Community-based solutions are unique to the location, but tend to advocate community intervention in intimate partner violence and tribal intolerance of violence against women (Ned-Sunyboy 2008). Smith (2012) suggests imagining long-term solutions that involve using traditional tribal customs to enhance community responses to intimate violence. That model of community accountability must not only hold offenders accountable for their actions, but ensure the safety of survivors (Smith 2005, 2012).

There are "community-based, culturally responsive" projects that have been piloted, in which traditional ways of teaching (e.g., using elders to teach nonviolent, respectful interactive values) and the use of traditional cultural healing practices have been implemented (Ned-Sunnyboy 2008). For example, the Alaska Native Women's Resource Center (2019) developed a training curriculum for Native villages in Alaska, in which intimate partner violence is discussed and traditional, community-based responses are introduced. The responses maximize victim safety and encourage intervention to hold offenders accountable as well as teach tribal values regarding gender and violence (Alaska Native Women's Resource Center 2019).

Strengthening the prosecution of intimate partner violence, then, should be combined with tribal development of long-term, community-based solutions that enhance offender accountability and victim safety (Smith 2012). In American and Canadian Indigenous communities, traditional (pre-colonization) tribal values included respect for women and the importance of women's roles in the community (Baskin 2020; Ned-Sunnyboy 2008). Part of the healing process for Indigenous communities is to restore those values to the tribe, and to incorporate them into the response to intimate violence (Giesbrecht et al. 2022; Ned-Sunnyboy 2008; Oden and Balog-Patrick 2024). Based on these concerns, the National Domestic Violence Hotline and the National Indigenous Women's Resource Center created StrongHearts Native Helpline, which is staffed with trained Native advocates (Begay 2020). It was important that the hotline be staffed by Native advocates, because non-Native advocates would not understand how the close connections to kin and the tribal community would prevent a victim from reporting intimate violence

(Begay 2020; Meyer and Stambe 2021). "It's immensely critical that advocates are able to empathize with the struggle to find help in close-knit communities where there is an imminent fear of judgement or rejection from one's own friends and family" (Begay 2020: 3).

Smith (2005) recommends the following improvements to policy: Interventions should address both interpersonal violence and state violence so that the intersectionality of personal and structural challenges is part of the response. "Safety for battered women is more than just stopping the physical violence; it also encompasses a woman's ability to be and act sovereign...She should receive comfort and support from her community. In addition, the tribe must ensure that offenders are held accountable for the violence they perpetrate. Tribal civil and criminal justice systems must provide effective intervention without exceptions for relationship or community status. Above all, there must be a strong message that the community will not tolerate the use of violence" (Ybanez 2008: 59).

This model of community accountability has implications for sheltering Indigenous survivors of intimate partner violence. There are few shelters specifically for Native American victims of intimate partner violence (Begay 2020; Ybanez 2008). Tribal communities tend to be small, and, given the rurality of most of these communities and the distance to law enforcement, a remote, confidential shelter would be difficult to protect. "Shelters" as such, need to be in a place where there is community, witnesses, and tribal elders who can intervene in an offender's behavior.

Research suggests that Indigenous women favor a hybrid model of restorative justice and tribal practices with the criminal justice system as backup (Coker 2006; Nancarrow 2006). For example, peacemaking in the Navajo justice system incorporates Navajo beliefs about "gender harmony," familial support, and traditional "horizontal" conceptions of justice to try to change the perpetrator and compensate the victim (Coker 2006). In this same study, victim advocates criticized the peacemaking process for battered women, because (a) some victims are in high-risk situations, and this model does not offer enough protection for them; (b) the narrative around partner violence can be dismissive, as if it was simply a disagreement, and peacemaking leans toward preserving marriage; and (c) victims' needs are secondary to the rehabilitative needs of the offender (Coker 2006). Given victim advocate objections to peacemaking and restorative justice, Coker (2006) suggests a hybrid model that supports peacemaking with a criminal justice system that collaborates with Navajo justice systems as well as domestic violence victim advocates. Non-Indigenous women, in fact, are more likely to favor the use of the criminal justice system with restorative justice as an alternative (Nancarrow 2006). In this study, Indigenous women objected to the criminal justice approach to intimate partner violence, because the perspectives of Indigenous people were not incorporated into the response, and actually escalated violence against women while separating Indigenous families. This was viewed as a continuation of colonizing policies that historically had decimated Indigenous families (Nancarrow 2006).

In conclusion, community-based solutions to intimate partner violence in Indigenous communities must incorporate tribal perspectives into policies and practices in order to address multiple layers of trauma in victims and their communities.

REFERENCES

18 U.S.C. 1153. 1885. *The Major Crimes Act: Offenses Committed within Indian Country.*

Agtuca, Jacqueline. 2008. Beloved women: Life givers, caretakers, teachers of future generations. In *Sharing our stories of survival: Native women surviving violence*, ed. S. Deer, B. Clairmont, C.A. Martell, and M.L. White Eagle, 3–27. Lanham: Altamira Press.

Alaska Native Women's Resource Center. 2019. *Curriculum materials.* Retrieved 3 June 2024 at https://www.aknwrc.org/our-work/alaska-curriculum/curriculum-materials/.

American Probation and Parole Association. 2009. *Community Corrections Response to Domestic Violence: Guidelines for Practice.* Washington, D.C.: Office on Violence Against Women, Office of Justice Programs, U.S. Department of Justice.

Amnesty International. 2007. *Maze of Injustice: The Failure to Protect Indigenous Women from Sexual Violence in the USA.* Amnesty International Publications. Retrieved 27 Feb 2018 at www.amnestyusa.org/pdfs/mazeofinjustice.pdf.

Arnull, Elaine, and Stacey Stewart. 2021. Developing a theoretical framework to discuss mothers experiencing domestic violence and being subject to interventions: A cross-national perspective. *International Journal for Crime, Justice and Social Democracy* 10 (2): 113–126.

Bachman, Ronet, Heather Zaykowski, Rachel Kallmyer, Margarita Poteyeva, and Christina Lanier. 2008. *Violence against American Indian and Alaska native women and the criminal justice response: What is known."* NCJ223691. Washington, DC: National Institute of Justice.

Baskin, Cyndy. 2020. Contemporary Indigenous women's roles: Traditional teachings or internalized colonialism? *Violence against Women* 26 (15–16): 2083–2101.

Begay, Chrystal and Tinesha Zandamela. 2018. *Sexual assault on Native American reservations in the U.S.* Ballard Brief. Retrieved 31 May 2024 at https://static1.squarespace.com/static/5f088a46ebe405013044f1a4/t/64f 773ce5ef35a61a9512003/1693938640297/BegayZandamelaPDF.docx.pdf.

Begay, Maurita. 2020. *Domestic violence advocacy service created by Natives for Natives.* The Circle: Native American News and Art. Retrieved 31 July 2023 at https://thecirclenews.org/health/domestic-violence-advocacy-service-created-by-natives-for-natives.

Bosch, Kathy, and Walter R. Schumm. 2004. Accessibility to resources: Helping rural women in abusive partner relationships become free from abuse. *Journal of Sex & Marital Therapy* 30 (5): 357–370.

Heart, Brave, Maria Yellow Horse, and Lemyra M. DeBruyn. 1998. The American Indian holocaust: Healing historical unresolved grief. *American Indian & Alaska Native Mental Health Research* 8 (2): 60–82.

Burnette, Catherine. 2015a. From the ground up: Indigenous women's after violence experiences with the formal service system in the United States. *The British Journal of Social Work* 45: 1526–1545.

Burnette, Catherine. 2015b. Historical oppression and intimate partner violence experienced by indigenous women in the United States: Understanding connections. *Social Service Review* 89 (3): 54–67.

Burrage, Rachel L., MaryBeth Gagnon, and Sandra A. Graham-Bermann. 2021. Trauma history and social support among American Indian/Alaska Native and non-Native survivors of intimate partner violence. *Journal of Interpersonal Violence* 36 (5–6): 3326–3345.

Clairmont, Bonnie. 2008. Overview of sexual violence perpetrated by purported Indian medicine men. In *Sharing our stories of survival: Native women surviving violence*, ed. S. Deer, B. Clairmont, C.A. Martell, and M.L. White Eagle, 215–228. Lanham: Altamira Press.

Clairmont, Bonnie, and Sarah Deer. 2008. Introduction to advocacy for Native women who have been raped. In *Sharing our stories of survival: Native women surviving violence*, ed. S. Deer, B. Clairmont, C.A. Martell, and M.L. White Eagle, 181–190. Lanham: Altamira Press.

Clark, Rose L., and Carrie L. Johnson. 2008. Overview of issues facing native women who are survivors of violence in urban communities. In *Sharing our stories of survival: Native women surviving violence*, ed. S. Deer, B. Clairmont, C.A. Martell, and M.L. White, 87–99. Lanham: Altamira Press.

Coker, Donna. 2006. Restorative justice, Navajo peacemaking and domestic violence. *Theoretical Criminology* 10 (1): 67–85.

Crichton-Hill, Yvonne, and Annabel Taylor. 2013. Intimate partner violence. In *Understanding violence: context and practice in the human services*, ed. A. Taylor and M. Connolly, 102–117. Christchurch: Canterbury University Press.

Deer, Sarah. 2015. *The beginning and ending of rape: Confronting sexual violence in native America*. Minneapolis: University of Minnesota Press.

Donovan, R., L. Wood, G. Jalleh, and P. Ivery. 2010. *Help break down the wall' community attitudes survey: Summary and results*. Retrieved 3 June 2024 at http://www.preventingchildabuse.com.au/public/pdfs/NAPCAN_Survey_Report_Final_4_June_2010.pdf.

Duran, Eduardo, Bonnie Duran, Wilbur Woodis, and Pamela Woodis. 1998. A postcolonial perspective on domestic violence in Indian Country. In *Family violence and men of color*, ed. R. Carrillo and J. Tello, 143–162. New York: Springer.

Durst, Douglas. 1991. Conjugal violence: Changing attitudes in two northern Native communities. *Community Mental Health Journal* 27: 359–373.

Ferraro, Kathleen J. 2006. *Neither Angels Nor Demons: Women, crime, and victimization*. Boston: Northeastern University Press.

Fotheringham, Sarah, Lana Wells, and Sharon Goulet. 2021. Strengthening the circle: An international review of government domestic violence prevention plans and inclusion of Indigenous peoples. *Violence against Women* 27 (3–4): 425–446.

Gauthier, G. Robin., Sara C. Fracisco, Gilal Khan, and Kirk Dombrowski. 2021. Social integration and domestic violence support in an indigenous community: Women's recommendations of formal versus informal sources of support. *Journal of Interpersonal Violence* 36 (7–8): 3117–3141.

Giesbrecht, Crystal J., Laleh Jamshidi, Carrie LaVallie, JoLee Sasakamoose, and R. Nicholas Carleton. 2022. Assessing the efficacy of a cultural and artistic intervention for Indigenous women who have experienced intimate partner violence. *Violence against Women* 28 (14): 3375–3399.

Gilbert, Sheena L., Emily M. Wright, and Tara N. Richards. 2021. Decolonizing VAWA 2021: A step in the right direction for protecting Native American women. *Feminist Criminology* 16 (4): 447–460.

Gurm, Balbir, and Jennifer Marchbank. 2020. Why survivors don't report. In *Making sense of a global pandemic: relationship violence and working together towards a violence free society*, ed. B. Gurm, G. Salgado, J. Marchbank, and S. Early. Surrey: Kwantlen Polytechnic University.

Hamby, Sherry. 2000. The importance of community in a feminist analysis of domestic violence among American Indians. *American Journal of Community Psychology* 28: 649–669.

Heidinger, Loanna. 2021. *Intimate partner violence: Experiences of First Nations, Métis and Inuit women in Canada, 2018*. Statistics Canada. Retrieved 30

May 2024 at https://www150.statcan.gc.ca/n1/pub/85-002-x/2021001/article/00007-eng.htm.

Hill, Brenda. 2008. "The role of advocates in the tribal legal system: Context is everything." In *Sharing Our Stories of Survival: Native Women Surviving Violence* ed. S Deer, B Clairmont, CA Martell, and ML White Eagle. 193–213. Lanham, MD: Altamira Press.

Holt, Marilyn Irvin. 2001. *Indian orphanages*. Lawrence: University Press of Kansas.

Humpage, Louise. 2005. Tackling indigenous disadvantage in the twenty-first century: 'Social inclusion' and Māori in New Zealand. In *Indigenous peoples & poverty: An international perspective*, ed. R. Eversole, J.-A. McNeish, and A.D. Cimadamore, 158–183. New York: St. Martin's Press.

Jolly, Margaret. 2012. Engendering violence in Papua New Guinea: Persons, power and perilous transformations. In *Engendering violence in Papua New Guinea*, ed. M. Jolly, C. Stewart, and C. Brewer, 1–45. Canberra: ANU E Press.

Jones, Ashley Minner. 2024. A monumental statement. *American Indian Spring* 25 (1): 42–43.

Jones, Loring. 2008. The distinctive characteristics and needs of domestic violence victims in a Native American community. *Journal of Family Violence* 23: 113–118.

Keomoungkhoun, Nataly. 2020. *Dispersed but still defiant: What happened to North Texas' Native American tribes?* Dallas Morning News 26 Dec, B1–2.

Krug, Etienne G., Linda L. Dahlberg, James A. Mercy, Anthony B. Zwi, and Rafael Lozano, eds. 2002. *World report on violence and health*. Geneva: World Health Organization.

LaPointe, Charlene Ann. 2008. Sexual violence: An int.roduction to the social and legal issues for native women. In *Sharing Our Stories of Survival: Native Women Surviving Violence* ed. S Deer, B Clairmont, CA Martell, ML White Eagle. 31–46. Lanham, MD: AltaMira Press.

Luna-Gordinier, Anne. 2018. Stalking in Indian country: Enhancing tribal sovereignty through the Tribal Law and Order Act and the Violence Against Women Act. In *Crime and social justice in Indian Country*, ed. M.O. Nielsen and K. Jarratt-Snider, 121–141. Tucson: The University of Arizona Press.

Mann, Charles C. 2022. *We Are Here*. National Geographic Magazine. July: 36–75.

McNeish, John Andrew, and Robyn Eversole. 2005. Introduction: Indigenous peoples and poverty. In *Indigenous peoples & poverty: An international perspective*, ed. R. Eversole, J.-A. McNeish, and A.D. Cimadamore, 1–26. New York: St. Martin's Press.

Merry, Sally Engle. 2006. *Human rights & gender violence: Translating international law into local justice*. Chicago: The University of Chicago Press.

Meyer, Silke, and Rose-Marie. Stambe. 2021. Indigenous women's experiences of domestic and family violence, help-seeking and recovery in regional Queensland. *The Australian Journal of Social Issues* 56 (3): 443–458.

Ministry of Social Development. 2009. *Campaign overview: Campaign for action on family violence.* Wellington, NZ. Retrieved 5 May 2014 from www.areyouok.org.nz/files/news/Campaign_Overview.pcf.

Mirsky, Laura. 2003. *Family group conferencing worldwide: Part one in a series.* Restorative Practices Eforum. Retrieved 4 June 2024 at www.restorativepractices.org.

Mullighan, Edward. 2008. *Children on Anangu Pitjantjatjara Yankunytjatjara (APY) Lands Commission of Inquiry: A report into sexual abuse.* Children in State Care and Children on APY Lands Commission of Inquiry. Retrieved 3 June 2024 at https://www.anangu.com.au/en/apy-information/reports-about-the-apy-lands/729-mullighan-inquiry-report-apy-lands/file.

Nancarrow, Heather. 2006. In search of justice for domestic and family violence: Indigenous and non-Indigenous Australian women's perspectives. *Theoretical Criminology* 10 (1): 87–106.

Ned-Sunnyboy, Eleanor. 2008. "Special issues facing Alaska Native women survivors of violence." In *Sharing Our Stories of Survival: Native Women Surviving Violence* ed. S Deer, B Clairmont, CA Martell, and ML White Eagle. 71–84. Lanham, MD: Altamira Press.

Oetzel, John, and Bonnie Duran. 2004. Intimate partner violence in American Indian and/or Alaska Native communities: A social ecological framework of determinants and interventions. *American Indian and Alaska Native Mental Health Research* 11 (3): 49–68.

Oliphant v. Suquamish Indian Tribe 435 U.S. (191, 210), 1978.

Oxfam. 2023. *Women's rights and gender justice: Ending poverty and injustice starts with gender justice and rights for women.* Retrieved 18 Jan 2023 at https://www.oxfamamerica.org/explore/issues/womens-rights-and-gender-justice/.

Pennell, Joan, and Stephanie Francis. 2005. Safety conferencing: Toward a coordinated and inclusive response to safeguard women and children. *Violence against Women* 11 (5): 666–692.

Perry, Steven W. 2022. *Tribal crime data collection activities, 2022.* Bureau of Justice Statistics, July. Washington, D.C.: U.S. Department of Justice.

Price, Joshua M. 2012. *Structural violence: Hidden brutality in the lives of women.* Albany: State University of New York Press.

Public Law 83-280, 67 Stat. 588(1953).

Renzetti, Claire M. 1992. *Violent betrayal: Partner abuse in lesbian relationships.* Newbury Park: Sage Publications Inc.

Rosay, Andre B. 2016. *Violence against American Indian and Alaska Native women and men: 2010 findings from the National Intimate Partner and Sexual*

Violence Survey. National Institute of Justice Research Report. Retrieved 28 Apr 2024 at https://www.ojp.gov/pdffiles1/nij/249736.pdf.

Shepherd, Judy. 2001. Where do you go when its 40 below? Domestic violence among rural Alaska Native women. *Journal of Women and Social Work* 16 (4): 488–510.

Smith, Andrea. 2005. *Conquest: Sexual Violence and American Indian Genocide*. Cambridge, MA: South End Press.

Smith, Andrea. 2012. Decolonizing anti-rape law and strategizing accountability in Native American communities. *Social Justice* 37 (4): 36–43.

Sudderth, Lori K. 2017. Bringing in 'The Ones Who Know Them': Informal community and safety planning for victims of intimate partner violence in New Zealand. *Violence against Women*. 23 (2): 222–242.

Taylor, Natalie and Jenny Mouzos. 2006. *Community attitudes to violence against women survey 2006: A full technical report*. Melbourne: VicHealth.

Taylor, Natalie and Judy Putt. 2007. *Adult sexual violence in Indigenous and culturally and linguistically diverse communities in Australia*. Trends and Issues in Crime and Criminal Justice. Canberra: Australian Government, Australian Institute of Criminology.

The Indian Civil Rights Act of 1968 (ICRA), 25 U.S.C. 1301-1304.

Tjaden, Patricia, and Nancy Thoennes. 2000. *Full report of the prevalence, incidence, and consequences of violence against women: Findings form the National Violence Against Women Survey*. Washington: U.S. Department of Justice.

Twiss, George. 2008. The role of probation in providing safety for native women. In *Sharing Our Stories of Survival: Native Women Surviving Violence* ed. S Deer, B Clairmont, CA Martell, and ML White Eagle. 311–334. Lanham, MD: Altamira Press.

UN Women. 2022. *UN Committee calls on states to protect the rights of Indigenous women and girls*. Retrieved 30, June 2023 at https://www.ohchr.org/en/documents/general-comments-and-recommedations/general-recommendation-no39-2022-rights-indigenous.

Violence Against Women Reauthorization Act of 2005. U.S. Public Law 109–162. 109th Congress, 5 January 2006.

Violence Against Women Reauthorization Act of 2013. U.S. Public Law 113–114. 113th Congress, 7 March 2013.

Violence Against Women Reauthorization Act of 2022. U.S. Public Law 117–103. 117th Congress, 15 March 2022.

Wands, Zoë Elspeth., and Tolib Mirzoev. 2022. Intimate partner violence against indigenous women in Sololá, Guatemala: Qualitative insights into perspectives of service providers. *Violence against Women* 28 (1): 150–168.

Weaver, Hilary N. 2009. The colonial context of violence: Reflections on violence in the lives of Native American women. *Journal of Interpersonal Violence* 24 (9): 1552–1563.

Weldon, S. Laurel. 2002. *Protest, policy, and the problem of violence against women: A cross-national comparison.* Pittsburgh: University of Pittsburgh Press.

Wild, Rex and Patricia Anderson. 2007. *Ampe Akelyernemane Meke Mekarle: Little Children are Sacred.* Report of the Northern Territory Board of Inquiry into the Protection of Aboriginal Children from Sexual Abuse. Retrieved 3 June 2024 at https://humanrights.gov.au/sites/default/files/57.4%20%E2% 80%9CLittle%20Children%20are%20Sacred%E2%80%9D%20report.pdf.

Willis, Matthew. 2010. *Community safety in Australian Indigenous communities: Service providers' perceptions.* Research and Public Policy Series no. 110. Canberra: Australian Institute of Criminology.

Willis, Matthew. 2011. *Non-disclosure of violence in Australian Indigenous communities.* Trends & Issues in Crime and Criminal Justice No. 405, Australian Institute of Criminology.

Women's Justice Initiative [WJI]. 2022. *Indigenous women transforming communities: Leading for a lasting impact.* In 2022 Annual Report Women's Justice Initiative. Retrieved 28 May 2024 at https://womens-justice.org/wjis-2022-annual-report-is-here/.

Ybanez, Victoria. 2008. "Domestic violence: An introduction to the social and legal issues for Native women." In *Sharing Our Stories of Survival: Native Women Surviving Violence* ed. S Deer, B Clairmont, CA Martell, and ML White Eagle. 49–67. Lanham, MD: Altamira Press.

Yüyan, Kiliii. 2022. "Raising voices." *National Geographic: Pictures of the Year.* December.

Zorn, Jean G. 2012. Engendering violence in the Papua New Guinea courts: Sentencing in rape trials. In *Engendering violence in Papua New Guinea*, ed. M. Jolly, C. Stewart, and C. Brewer, 163–195. Canberra: ANU E Press.

CHAPTER 5

Conclusions: Wearing Away the Stone

Abstract The final chapter describes programming that addresses intimate partner violence, either directly or indirectly, in low-income, tight-knit communities around the world. The initiatives described here drive the recommendations for future programming in these settings. The recommendations include (1) to empower and invest in women and girls through training and financing; (2) to educate men and boys, community leaders, and frontline workers to change the response to intimate partner violence; (3) to build collaborative, victim-centered, trauma-informed support services for survivors; (4) to use digital technology and social media to the extent possible for connection with other survivors, communication with support services, and educational programming about intimate partner violence. The chapter ends with a call for more research on violence against women in remote areas and support for community-based responses to intimate partner violence.

Keywords Intimate partner violence · Domestic violence · Social support · Digital technology · Social media · Education · Training · Informal support · Community-based advocacy · Men/boys and programming · Gender norms · Women's rights · Low-income countries · Rural · Tribal · Island · Empowerment · Collaborative

© The Author(s), under exclusive license to Springer Nature Switzerland AG 2024
L. K. Sudderth, *Changing Communities in Challenging Contexts to Address Intimate Partner Violence*,
https://doi.org/10.1007/978-3-031-75356-5_5

"Keep Dropping Water on the Stone, and Eventually, it Wears Away."—Tine Ward, CEO, Rockflower

During an ethical review of one of my studies on intimate partner violence, a member of the Institutional Review Board asked incredulously, "Why would anyone *want* to answer these questions?" More than one expert, in fact, had cautioned me that experiences of intimate partner violence are private, and few women would talk to me about it. My research in Saint Lucia, Costa Rica, and Nicaragua left me with the opposite impression: in places where there are few venues for women to discuss the abuse in their lives, they may, indeed, welcome the opportunity to talk about it, even with a stranger. The challenge is to match that eagerness for disclosure with programming that leads to meaningful change.

International studies recommend programming that addresses the predictors of intimate partner violence, including child maltreatment, alcohol misuse, the lack of healthy communication skills, gender and income inequality, the spotty regulation of weapons, women's unemployment, legal barriers to leaving an abusive relationship, norms supporting violence, and attitudes about family violence (Jewkes et al. 2002; UN Women 2013; World Health Organization 2022). This is in addition to strengthening the criminal justice response and social support for survivors of IPV. Some of the organizations profiled in this book do not have intimate partner violence at the center of their agenda, but the programs, the trainings, and the funding address those predictors, and thus impact violence in the community. Islands, rural areas, and tribal communities share characteristics that make disclosure and reporting of IPV challenging; escape is complicated by geography, a history of colonization, and comfort firmly rooted in family and friends. The cultural contexts, the gendered distribution of power and privilege, and the level of resources available vary, making each community unique in its limits and possibilities. The following lessons learned, therefore, are not formulaic, but represent a range of options inspired by research as well as examples from the field.

Empower and Invest in Women and Girls

Empowerment programming varies by the organization and the community setting, but it can refer to individual-level or community-level efforts to address violence; the program may target survivors of intimate partner violence, all women and girls, or both. On the individual level, empowerment is embodied in a supportive response to survivors of any type of violence or trauma that seeks to restore their sense of control over their lives. This is typically a component of safety planning or therapy for victims of intimate partner violence (Davies et al. 1998; Van der Kolk 2014). Organizations that work in challenging contexts recognize that individual support for victims is necessary but insufficient; the context in which survivors make decisions must also change. Empowerment programming ranges from educational initiatives to inform women and girls about their civil rights and their potential as community leaders to creating employment opportunities for rural and Indigenous women (New Haven/León Sister City Project 2021; Raise Your Voice Saint Lucia, Inc. 2024; Women's Justice Initiative 2024).

Economic empowerment for survivors of IPV recognizes that women who leave abusive relationships need to be able to support themselves and their families financially. In response, Raise Your Voice Saint Lucia, Inc. is building an agro-processing facility that will train and employ survivors of IPV, including LGBTQI survivors, with the goal of increasing their "economic and emotional resilience" using produce native to the island (Raise Your Voice Saint Lucia, Inc. 2024). There will be additional training opportunities in management, and RYVSL has already awarded small grants to women, girls, and LGBTQI community members to start their own businesses in line with the agro-processing facility.

The Women's Justice Initiative (WJI) is based in Guatemala, and it is focused on empowering Indigenous rural women to be leaders in their communities and to have the resources to address intimate partner violence (Women's Justice Initiative 2024). Like other rural and tribal communities around the world, this is a place where it is difficult to report intimate partner violence and remain anonymous. There is cultural and religious pressure to marry early and to remain in a marriage, even if it includes abuse; and reporting a violent spouse has consequences because of the gendered social structure, the acceptance of machismo, and victim blaming, according to Dr. Mary Catherine Driese,[1] Impact and Development Officer at WJI. She pointed out that most victims of IPV prefer mediation or a peaceful separation from their spouse, but

---

[1] I spoke with Dr. Driese through a zoom interview, 13 June 2024.

without legal or economic support, this is not possible. The Women's Justice Initiative, with 38 employees, offers four programs to rural indigenous women, including free legal guidance from paralegals and attorneys who speak their language and come from their culture; they can also arrange and facilitate mediation, with the understanding that victim safety is paramount. Second, WJI offers leadership and human rights training, which helps women to become advocates and leaders in their communities. Third, they offer a separate training to adolescent girls about the importance of delaying marriage for improved chances at education, better health, and personal goals. Fourth, WJI offers a women's rights education program that includes legal literacy, domestic violence, and other skill-building workshops (Women's Justice Initiative 2024). Evaluation results suggested that the project was successful in that girls who took part in the program were less likely to marry before the age of 18. WJI was also successful in facilitating more access to justice, better collaboration, and reaching out to community leaders, who then created action plans to reduce gender-based violence (Magoga 2019).

Rockflower is a philanthropic organization that supports community-based projects that recognize the leadership capabilities of women in finding solutions to social problems. Tine Ward,[2] CEO and founder, pointed out that because women take care of children, they are keen witnesses to social problems and eager to find solutions. So, Rockflower grants venture capital to projects led by social entrepreneurs and grassroots, women-led organizations; the projects empower, include, acknowledge, and sustain women and benefit their communities, and this has an impact on intimate partner violence. As the projects become profitable, they are able to expand, providing employment, leadership opportunities, and education for women and girls (Rockflower 2024).

For example, Rockflower partnered with the Foundation for Women and Children Empowerment (FOWACE) to fund a Village Savings and Loan Association project in rural Liberia that gave women in the village financial training and the materials needed for saving money for their children's education, medical care, and small business loans. Rockflower funding made it possible to initiate a soap-making business, and to purchase soap products and rice during the COVID-19 pandemic (Rockflower 2020). These initiatives reduce the vulnerability of women to

---

[2] Ms. Ward spoke to me in a zoom interview and over email about the philosophy behind Rockflower projects in June of 2024.

gendered victimization, because they have viable means for supporting themselves and their children. In addition, the women gained valuable emotional support talking to each other during the meetings, including discussions about their experiences with violence.

Education and Training for Women is Empowering, but Programming Should Include Men and Boys, Community Leaders, and Frontline Workers

Even in countries with progressive domestic violence legislation, rural women, women in remote tribal communities, and women with lower educational levels may not have the legal background to understand their civil rights under the law. In Saint Lucia, 39% of the women we interviewed had not gone beyond primary school, and several participants said they had dropped out of school to work or care for younger children. I heard similar stories in Goyena, Nicaragua, a rural village outside of León. When a social worker came to Goyena to facilitate a women's group, she pointed out that there was now a law against a man hitting his wife. The women laughed, incredulous that such a law could be implemented; but over the course of a year, they discussed their legal options with an attorney, learned about the feminist movement in Nicaragua, and took part in activities that inspired self-reflection on their lives as rural women. This, in turn, sparked discussion in their families, their friends, and beyond, and the tolerance of gendered violence in the village dissipated. Word travels fast in small communities, and by the time I visited Goyena, four years after the project had begun, women in nearby villages had asked for their own discussion groups (see Sudderth 2020).

Education and training are key to addressing intimate partner violence in challenging and remote locations. Educational programs can promote the prevention of intimate partner violence and/or improve the response to intimate partner violence. In my research, this type of programming was divided into (a) educational opportunities for survivors of IPV to increase their chances to successfully move away from abusive relationships and support themselves and their children; (b) programming to sensitize and coordinate the frontline points of response to IPV, as well as influential community members; and (c) programming to prevent intimate partner violence, targeting young women and girls, men and boys, as well as community leaders to change the norms and opportunity structures that support IPV. There are also programs that train community members to act as the frontline response to gender-based violence. For example, Oxfam Philippines partnered with United Youth of the Philippines (UnYPhil), a youth group, to create volunteer gender-based watch groups that assist survivors of gender-based violence and raise awareness (Oxfam 2022).

The Women's Project in Goyena, Nicaragua is an example of an educational program aimed at survivors of IPV, because most of the women had at least some experience with violence by a male partner; but the project also focused on the prevention of gender-based violence, and young girls often attended the open-air meetings with their mothers. The discussions with women and girls challenged stereotypes and explained civil rights (Sudderth 2020). Similarly, the Women's Rights Education Program run by the Women's Justice Initiative offers rural Indigenous women in Guatemala courses in legal literacy that result in more official reports of gender-based violence and requests for legal assistance from women who are victims of intimate partner violence (Women's Justice Initiative 2024).

In addition to offering education to survivors of IPV, social support may come from training community health workers, mental health providers, front-line workers in safety planning strategies, empowerment, and responding sensitively to disclosures of intimate partner violence (Devries et al. 2013; Nikupeteri, Skaffari, and Laitinen 2022; Wood et al. 2021). Raise Your Voice Saint Lucia, Inc. offered full-day workshops to frontline workers on trauma-informed, survivor-centered responses to disclosures of sexual violence and domestic violence, as well as a two-day workshop on effective multiagency collaboration to improve the response to gender-based violence. The audience included police officers, nurses, social workers, counselors, as well as community activists. Although the project was not evaluated, initial reports suggested an improved, streamlined, collaborative protocol for disclosures of gender-based violence. This type of training should be done regularly as new employees fill the positions of those who have been through the workshops.

The Women's Justice Initiative offers a two-year program to train Mayan women in leadership and community advocacy; these advocates then work with community leaders to improve the response to disclosures of gender-based violence (Women's Justice Initiative 2024). Educating community leaders often generates resistance, but it is a necessary part of the process (zoom interview, M.C. Driese, Impact and Development Officer, Women's Justice Initiative, 13 June 2024). Similarly, Raising

Her Voice in Nepal, which was sponsored by Oxfam, set up Community Discussion Classes (CDCs) with marginalized, low-income women to develop their awareness of their civil rights, including their rights under domestic violence legislation in Nepal, but also to encourage their participation in the decision-making sectors of their communities (Hopkins and Shrestha 2012). An evaluation of the program suggested that women who had taken part in the CDCs were more vocal in speaking up about their rights, but their communities also had an increased awareness of violence against women and discriminatory practices (Green 2015).

In addition to changing the response to IPV, educational programming is designed to prevent intimate partner violence. The Women's Justice Initiative, for example, offers a Girls Empowerment, Rights, and Leadership course, which is a six-month program for adolescent girls (WJI 2024). During the course, girls learn about their rights, discuss their goals in life, and learn about the importance of delaying marriage. Early marriage for girls is associated with a higher risk of intimate partner violence (Kidman 2016), so WJI also works with parents and community leaders to be supportive of later marriage for girls. Oxfam also recognized the significance of delaying marriage for girls in "Creating Spaces," a five-year project in the Philippines and five other countries[3] to change social norms that support child marriage and violence against women. In the Philippines, one project used both social media and on-the-ground community outreach to successfully challenge gender norms and beliefs about violence against women (Holland 2022). In addition, Oxfam Philippines partnered with other island organizations to deliver skills training, confidence building, and awareness raising, for example, on the impact of child marriage; some of the programming involved mothers and children, which very effectively increased the discussion of violence against women and the willingness of women to be advocates in their families and their communities (Holland 2022).

Nevertheless, the most effective interventions in reducing intimate partner violence include men and boys in their programming (Alsina et al. 2024; Eves 2006; Flood 2003; Stern and Niyibizi 2018). Community projects that include men may offer alternative constructions of nonviolent masculinity through media, workshops, or role models, using culturally appropriate ways to communicate these messages (Eves 2006;

---

[3] Indonesia, Nepal, Bangladesh, India, and Pakistan.

Flood 2003). According to Eves (2006), men should be encouraged to take a leading role in stopping other men from perpetrating violence against women.

Men as Partners was developed by EngenderHealth and the United Nations Population Fund (UNPF) to improve health by challenging gender norms, including gender-based violence (EngenderHealth and UNPF 2017). The premise of the program is that gender inequality and traditional attitudes about gender feed and inflame risky and problematic behaviors like having multiple sexual partners, substance abuse, and expressing dominance over women through violence. Men take part in workshops in which they are asked to reflect on gender norms and the negative effects of hegemonic masculinity, not only on women, but on their own health. Evaluations in multiple countries suggest that the program does lead to changes in attitudes about gender equity, specifically household decision-making, sharing of household duties, and justifications for intimate partner violence (Ditlopo et al. 2007; The CHAMPION Project. 2014; United Nations Population Fund 2009).

Other projects focus on a curriculum that targets the knowledge and communication skills of men and women in a relationship. *Indashyikirwa* in Rwanda, for example, is a five-month program for heterosexual couples who learn about intimate partner violence and alternative means for managing the behaviors associated with it (Stern and Niyibizi 2018). This course was in addition to increased support for reporting IPV and educating women about their legal rights and community leaders about appropriate responses to IPV disclosure. Some women received additional training in community advocacy. Interviews with participants suggested that the program sensitized them to the negative consequences of intimate partner violence, and resulted in men being less tolerant of IPV (Stern and Niyibizi 2018).

Build Collaborative, Victim-Centered, Trauma-Informed Support Services for Survivors

The practical needs of women trying to escape an abusive relationship are well-known to the professionals who work with them: housing, education, vocational training, jobs, childcare, legal services, counseling, medical attention, social support, sustenance, safety (Raise Your Voice Saint Lucia, Inc. 2024; Wilson and Kelsch 2024). The challenges of leaving an abusive relationship within the context of rurality, low anonymity, poverty, and strong kinship ties complicate the provision of services for survivors. NGOs and community organizations have wrestled with shelter, police response and prosecution, psychosocial support, transportation, and myriad details of life after IPV in places where it is almost impossible to slip away unnoticed. While the focus of international feminists has been on the role of government and legislation in responding to violence against women, there are potential uses of informal networks and communities to provide support for victims and hold offenders accountable (Kelly and Radford 1998; Kim 2011).

Internationally, survivor-centered, trauma-informed practices (e.g., listening to survivors, and incorporating their perspectives into policy and programming) are recommended to achieve justice for survivors of gender-based violence (International Development Law Organization [IDLO] and The Global Women's Institute 2022). As Dr. Driese from the Women's Justice Initiative, told me, "The victims define justice for themselves" (zoom interview, M.C. Driese, WIJ, 13 June 2024). In many of these remote communities, in fact, women do not want to leave the relationship, but they do want the violence to stop. Some organizations have, in fact, created collaborative opportunities for community members, in conjunction with social workers and criminal justice personnel, to monitor the behavior of the offender (e.g., Horn et al. 2016).

A shelter with a confidential address is not impossible, but much more difficult to bring about in these circumstances. For this reason, in some small towns in the United States and Australia, the domestic violence shelter is in the center of town, well-marked and obvious. If refuge is available, victims choose between staying in an abusive relationship in the community where they find their sustenance, comfort, and identity or going to a shelter, hidden from the abusive partner, but also isolated from the people who give them strength (Sudderth 2015).

One response to the challenge of finding refuge is to help the victim shelter in place, capitalizing on the social support she has in her community and creating a safety plan that takes into account her unique situation (Davies et al. 1998; Sabri et al. 2022; Sudderth 2015). The Women's Justice Initiative will, if necessary, find somewhere, most likely family, for a victim to stay until she can find permanent housing (zoom interview, M.C. Driese, 13 June 2024). Similarly, Raise Your Voice Saint Lucia, Inc. receives calls from women who need to leave their homes for their own safety. They will find refuge on the island, or there is an emergency protocol to transport women to another island. In Goyena, Nicaragua, there was no nearby shelter, but one of the women from the Women's Project had opened up her home as a temporary refuge.

Women who live in remote, rural, or tribal communities often do not have access to support groups where they can talk about the violence they have experienced. When I was surveying neighborhoods in St. Lucia about intimate partner violence, several survivors of IPV in one neighborhood said that they would like to speak to other women with similar experiences. Other researchers have also found that women's support or discussion groups are helpful for women to offer advice, safety planning, and emotional support to each other (Carrillo 1993; Eves 2006; Mkandawire-Valhmu et al. 2013; Sudderth 2015). In places where there are few counseling centers or mental health providers, it is important for women to find ways to talk to each other, whether that be a group facilitated by a social worker, a group organized by women trained to lead such initiatives, or digital groups that connect survivors from all over the world. Creating these communities or networks of support in person or online can offer survivors of intimate partner violence connection to other survivors, support groups, access to trained volunteers, and information about the dynamics of intimate partner violence (Campbell, Gray, and Brogden 2012; Goodman and Epstein 2008; White and Zora 2010).

The level of support from the community depends, of course, on not only the victim's relationships with her social network, but also the size of the community, the level of acceptance of interpersonal violence as normative, the cultural role of family in responding to crime, and the resources available in the vicinity (Goodman and Epstein 2008; Kelly and Radford 1998; Putnam 2000; Smith 2006). Mobilizing communities to address intimate partner violence is more effective when communities participate in creating the response (Merry 2006). An informed community is aware of the underlying factors that drive violence against women and are actively mobilized to prevent and respond in a way that increases support for victims of intimate violence and holds offenders accountable (Minckas, Shannon, and Mannell 2020; Sudderth 2015). Ultimately, intimate partner violence survivors must operate in safety, and they need supportive communities to move beyond the abuse (Abrahams 2010; Crichton-Hill 2013; Dasgupta n.d.).

Use Digital/Telecommunications to the Extent Possible

Survivors of intimate partner violence in rural locations, tribal communities, and small islands seldom report to authorities, at least partly because of the lack of anonymity in places where people tend to know each other. The #MeToo Movement has provided a virtual podium for 1.7 million survivors worldwide to speak out against sexual assault and harassment, and to demonstrate the ubiquity of this type of violence. For rural, Indigenous, and isolated women, digital technology, social media, and other internet-based supports allow them to get information, receive support, and tell their stories. The World Bank (2024) proposes online learning, vocational training, and digital literacy for women and girls as an anti-poverty initiative and as a way to fight violence against women. However, these benefits are dependent on the accessibility of technology in remote areas and women's access to technology.

The #MeToo movement altered the experience of survivors of gender-based violence, because, with internet access, they could now connect to others with similar experiences; moreover, they could reach out to other survivors without engaging conventional institutions or other community members, and they could find information about the violence they experienced and how to cope with it (Nomamiukor and Wisco 2024). There is disagreement on how to engage and empower survivors online (e.g., Núñez Puente et al. 2017), and there can be negative and hostile attacks in digital space; however, participating in discussions about gendered violence and other feminist topics is typically easier in social media (Mendes et al. 2018). Online, women can discuss and share feelings and personal narratives that defy traditional gender expectations (Adams et al. 2021; Pain 2021).

Social media has been used worldwide to encourage grassroots movements, particularly those with little hope of organizing through in-person meetings (Hanson and Gomez 2018). In Nicaragua, social media was used to mobilize student protests against the Ortega administration, which had not addressed destructive fires in the most biodiverse parts of the country (Alemán, nd). Through social media, the movement expanded from a student-based group to an alliance among a variety of groups opposing the Ortega administration, even though the movement itself remained rather loose in terms of structure (Hanson and Gomez 2018). Similarly, by using Twitter to share experiences and name perpetrators of sexual violence, women demanded social change (Pain

2021). In places where the criminal justice system has failed to address violence against women, social media and digital technology provide an alternative—e.g., making the perpetrator visible through social media, publicizing the lack of response from authorities, and putting social pressure on them to act (Dey 2020). In remote areas, information can be passed on via the internet. In a randomized controlled trial, Glass et al. (2017) compared internet-based personalized safety planning to a website that offered basic safety information. While there were no differences detected in mental health outcomes, intimate partner violence survivors who used individualized internet-based safety planning reported using more safety behaviors and were more likely to leave their abusive partner (Glass et al. 2017).

The internet opens up the conversation to everyone, regardless of location, status, or occupation—it allows women (particularly younger women) who are unaccustomed to speaking out to add their voices to the larger collective call for change (Dey 2020; Jackson 2018; Keller 2015). Using social media, specifically hashtag# tweets allows survivors to make brief statements about their experiences of intimate violence without identifying themselves, but still connecting to the wider community of survivors in the world (Mendes, Keller, and Ringrose 2018). Moreover, digital technology allows for the connection of survivors of intimate violence across national borders, oceans, indeed, around the world (Dey 2020). For women living in communities where people tend to know each other, for survivors of intimate partner violence who are isolated and fearful, the anonymity allowed by these platforms provides a passage for outreach in the comfort of safety.

There are, of course, limitations to the use of technology to address intimate partner violence in close-knit communities. Although Twitter and hashtag feminism give women around the world a place to voice their anger and their stories of gender-based violence, it is only those who have *access* to social media are represented (Núñez Puente et al. 2021; Pain 2021). For women and girls in many low-income countries, the priority is household duties and caring for young children, which excludes them from digital opportunities, digital skill acquisition, links to resources, and access to the internet. In addition, illiteracy and the diversity of languages may restrict who is able to find information on a phone and contribute to a larger conversation online (Kaplan 2006). In low-income countries and locations, it may be more common to pre-pay for phones or to share phones, which may limit women's access to the internet and social media

(Kaplan 2006). In the hands of an abusive spouse, a shared phone would restrict opportunities for survivors of intimate partner violence to use the internet undetected.

Technology is also a tool for abusive partners, and the online abuse of women is on the continuum of abusive behaviors that define intimate violence against women (DeKeseredy 2021; Kelly 1988). Abusive online behaviors include technological surveillance, hacking, humiliating the victim through social media, and robbing the victim of a sense of safety and privacy (Woodlock et al. 2023).

Furthermore, abuse through technology is often dismissed by law enforcement as less serious than physical violence or as a dysfunctional individual even though it is clearly part of a larger pattern of abusive behavior (Chan 2022; Woodlock et al. 2023). One study, in fact, suggested that risk assessments for violent extremism often overlook technological expressions of gender-based violence, even though the discourse clearly called for violence against women in response to an assumed threat to men (Chan 2022). Grimani et al. (2022) did a systematic review of the literature on digital technology use and intimate partner violence from 2004 to 2017. They found in 22 studies that survivors use technology to reach out for help and resources; they use technology to block the perpetrator or hide themselves. Perpetrators, however, use technology to stalk victims, to track their movements, often with Facebook or spyware, and because of this, victims may avoid an online presence.

Just as social media provides a community for survivors, perpetrators of gender-based violence and men who proclaim their hatred for women online may find each other through the internet (Furl 2022). Social media provides a community that allows users to favor themselves and their ingroup, while derogating outgroups, including women and marginalized groups; this reinforces stereotypes through community consensus (Furl 2022). Similarly, resistance to hashtag feminism in South Africa included responses that were victim blaming, and suggested that men often fail to examine the role of masculinity or patriarchy in gender-based violence. They instead blame women, suggest that not all men are the problem, or claim that hashtag feminism goes too far or doesn't go far enough (Reneses and Bosch 2023).

Beyond that, there is disagreement on the best methods for reaching survivors or changing community norms. A systematic review of mobile apps to address violence against women (released between 2010 and

2018) suggested that almost half of the apps were set up for emergency situations, a little over one-fifth functioned as educational tools, and smaller proportions of the apps were set up to report violent incidents (14%), to offer support to survivors (12%), or to enhance safety by avoiding "potential at-risk situations" (6%) (Eisenhut et al. 2020). While emergency apps represent an improvement over the past, they do not address the ongoing abuse that includes not only physical violence, but emotional abuse and coercive control; most apps focus on women, rather than male attitudes about women, thus responding to an emergency with more efficiency, but failing to address the bigger picture (See Eisenhut et al. 2020).

Nevertheless, the potential for using digital technology to reach remote survivors is undeniable, and there are, indeed, projects that have successfully overcome such barriers. Digital strategies, of course, have to account for limited connectivity, variations in levels of literacy and digital skills, and gender norms restricting women's access to technology. For example, in a rural part of India, where there was little internet connectivity and few women with smartphones, a local NGO collaborated with law enforcement to make the app Safecity available to women in the area. The app allowed the police to map reported experiences of gender-based violence; women in the area gathered at a local community to make those reports (Adams et al. 2021). Using digital technology to record their stories, and to learn more about their own civil rights, the women began to challenge patriarchal limits to their education, their vocational capabilities, even their daily routines (Adams et al. 2021). The program also allowed them to contribute to discussions on community efforts to improve women's safety, something rarely discussed before the introduction of the digital app (Adams et al. 2021).

Technology through the internet, social media, and digital formats has the potential to reach survivors of intimate partner violence anonymously in communities where people tend to know one another. It can provide information, community, support, and voice, all while giving choice to the survivor about when or how to identify herself as such. Guaranteeing women's unimpeded access to digital technology is one tool for raising awareness and moving toward safety.

Conclusions

Community involvement in keeping women safe from intimate partner violence ranges from minimal involvement, where survivors need to find their own way to safety through personal social networks, to the ideal community in which intimate partner violence is not tolerated, and the perpetrator is the one who must leave or be rehabilitated (Sudderth 2015). Ultimately, the challenge is to change the community to hold perpetrators accountable and support victims but also to rewrite the script of gendered expectations about who needs assistance. Martin and Hand (2006) argue that communities can be "informed individuals" who are intolerant of intimate partner violence and provide support to victims not only through refuge but through intervention. They point out that perpetrators in these communities will see their own behavior as deviant, and themselves in need of help. Communities should take responsibility for responding to violence against women so that victims will find support, regardless of where they turn for assistance (Martin and Hand 2006).

Communities, then, must be part of the movement to challenge structural violence that frames gendered violence as the prerogative of a male partner (Iadicola and Shupe 2003; Nikupeteri, Skaffari, and Laitinen 2022). This requires listening to victims' stories, providing awareness education to key leaders and the general population in communities, and working collaboratively to provide appropriate social support and services for victims (Nikupeteri, Skaffari, and Laitinen 2022). Local initiatives do not replace national legislation; rather they translate national laws and values into concrete steps (Merry 2006). Communities may respond to intimate partner violence as an aberration (i.e., intervene with the offender) or as indicative of larger structural inequalities. The former response does not address the latter, and the latter requires not only structural solutions, but community-level implementation.

It seems self-serving to say that all of this is worthy of research and evaluation. This is the type of research I enjoy and often get paid to conduct. But the point is well-taken that research and evaluation inform policy and protocol, training, and grant proposals. Research is needed to determine the effectiveness of safety planning for marginalized women, particularly Indigenous women, LGBTQ + women, and women in low-income countries (Sabri et al. 2022). Organizations serving victims in these areas benefit from evaluations and research that include both quantitative and qualitative data. Raise Your Voice Saint Lucia, Inc., Oxfam

International, and the Samoa Victim Support Group are examples of NGOs that actively work with social scientists to document experiences of violence in their communities, articulate cultural perspectives on violence and how to effectively end it, and evaluate their programming. Because of the remoteness of many of these communities and the demands of science and funding, it is tempting to focus on urban areas and larger, better-resourced communities. But the stories of IPV survivors in challenging contexts are portraits of resilience—women who calmly and courageously open their homes to other women who need refuge, women who describe unimaginable abuse and coercive control—and escape, women who emerge from disadvantage to save the lives of others. These are stories that should be recorded, so that others will know they are not alone and that there is hope for change.

References

Abrahams, Hilary. 2010. Life after leaving: Examining long-term outcomes for women escaping domestic abuse. *Te Awatea Review* 8 (1&2): 4–8.

Adams, Andrea, Suzanne G. Lea, and Elsa M. D'Silva. 2021. Digital technologies and interventions against gender-based violence in rural areas. *International Criminal Justice Review* 31 (4): 438–455.

Alemán, Amaru Ruíz. nd. *#SOSIndioMaiz: Environmental awareness awakens in Nicaragua*. Retrieved 23 Jan 2023 at https://www.peacebrigades.org/en/news/SOIndioMaiz.

Alsina, Ema, Joyce L. Browne, Desi Gielkens, Maaike A.J. Noorman, and John B.F. de Wit. 2024. Interventions to prevent intimate partner violence: A systematic review and meta-analysis. *Violence Against Women* 30(3-4):953–980.

Campbell, Lesley, Claire Gray, and Beryl Brogden. 2012. Peer support: Reframing the journey from lived experience of domestic violence. *Te Awatea Review* 10 (1-2): 18–22.

Carrillo, Roxanna. 1993. Violence against women: An obstacle to development. In *Women's lives and public policy*, ed. M. Turshen and B. Holcomb, 99–113. Westport: Greenwood Press.

Chan, Esli. 2022. Technology-facilitated gender-based violence, hate speech, and terrorism: A risk assessment on the rise of the Incel Rebellion in Canada. *Violence against Women* 29 (9): 1687–1718.

Crichton-Hill, Yvonne, and Annabel Taylor. 2013. Intimate partner violence. In *Understanding violence: Context and practice in the human services*, ed. A. Taylor and M. Connolly, 102–117. Christchurch: Canterbury University Press.

Dasgupta, Shamita D. n.d. *Creating sustainable safety for battered women*. Retrieved 6/19/13 from http://files.praxisinternational.org/2009/Safety_Eval_Ch_1_Women%27s_-Safety.pdf.

Davies, Jill, Eleanor Lyon, and D. Monti-Catania. 1998. *Safety planning with battered women: Complex lives/difficult choices*. Thousand Oaks: Sage Publications.

DeKeseredy, Walter S. 2021. *Woman abuse in rural places*. New York: Routledge.

Devries, Karen M., Joelle YT. Mak, Claudia Garcia-Moreno, Max Petzold, James C. Child, Gail Falder, Stephen Lim, et al. 2013. The global prevalence of intimate partner violence against women. *Science* 340: 1527–1528.

Dey, Adrija. 2020. Sites of exception: Gender violence, digital activism, and Nirbhaya's zone of anomie in India. *Violence against Women* 26 (11): 1423–1444.

Ditlopo, Prudence, Saiqa Mullick, Ian Askew, Ricardo Vernon, and Edwin Maroga, Sgidi Sibeko, Mokgethi Tshabalala, Rabbah Raletsemo, Dean Peacock, and Andrew Levack. 2007. *Testing the effectiveness of the Men as Partners program (MAP) in Soweto, South Africa*. Frontiers Final Report. Washington, D.C.: Population Council.

Eisenhut, Katharina, Ela Sauerborn, Claudia Garcia-Moreno, and Verina Wild. 2020. Mobile applications addressing violence against women: A systematic review. *BMJ Global Health* 5: 1–10.

EngenderHealth and United Nations Population Fund [UNFPA]. 2017. *Engaging men in sexual and reproductive health and rights, including family planning: Why using a gender lens matters*. Retrieved 10 June 2024 at https://www.engenderhealth.org/wp-content/uploads/imported-files/Engaging-Men-in-Sexual-and-Reproductive-Health-and-Rights-including-Family-Planning.pdf.

Eves, Richard. 2006. *Exploring the role of men and masculinities in Papua New Guienea in the 21st century: How to address violence in ways that generate empowerment for both men and women*. Report for Caritas Australia. Retrieved 15 January 2024 at: http://www.baha.com.pg/downloads/Masculinity%20and%20Violence%20in%20PNG.pdf.

Flood, Michael. 2003. Engaging men: Strategies and dilemmas in violence prevention education among men. *Women against Violence: An Australian Feminist Journal* 13: 25–32.

Furl, Katherine. 2022. Denigrating women, venerating 'Chad': Ingroup and outgroup evaluations among male supremacists on Reddit. *Social Psychology Quarterly* 85 (3): 279–299.

Glass, Nancy E., Nancy A. Perrin, Ginger C. Hanson, Tina L. Bloom, Jill T. Messing, Amber S. Clough, Jacquelyn C. Campbell, Andrea C. Gielen, James Case, and Karen B. Eden. 2017. The longitudinal impact of an internet safety decision aid for abused women. *American Journal of Preventive Medicine* 52 (5): 606–615.

Goodman, Linda A., and Deborah Epstein. 2008. *Listening to battered women: A survivor-centered approach to advocacy, mental health, and justice.* Washington: American Psychological Association.

Green, Duncan. 2015. *The raising her voice Nepal programme.* Oxford: Oxfam International.

Grimani, Aikaterini, Anna Gavine, and Wendy Moncur. 2022. An evidence synthesis of covert online strategies regarding intimate partner violence. *Trauma, Violence, & Abhe Rouse* 23 (2): 581–593.

Hanson, Lori and Miguel Gomez. 2018. *Deciphering the Nicaraguan student uprising.* NACLA 15 June. Retrieved 18 June 2018 at https://nacla.org/news/2018/06/15/decipherin-nicaraguan-student-uprising.

Holland, Jeremy. 2022. *Creating spaces to take action on violence against women and girls in the Philippines: Integrated impact evaluation report.* Oxford: Oxfam International.

Hopkins, Adrienne and Sandhya Shrestha. 2012. *Nothing is impossible: The Raising Her Voice programme in Nepal.* Oxford: Oxfam. https://oxfamlibr ary.com/bitstream/handle/10546/226735/pi-local-governance-nepal-250 52012.en.pdf;jsessionid=9D67BEFC3AD407EEB36EC1CB51E43CCD?seq uence=1.

Horn, Rebecca, Eve S. Puffer, Elisabeth Roesch, and Heidi Lehmann. 2016. 'I don't need an eye for an eye': Women's responses to intimate partner violence in Sierra Leone and Liberia. *Global Public Health* 11 (1–2): 108–121.

Iadicola, Peter, and Anson D. Shupe. 2003. *Violence, inequality, and human freedom.* Lanham: Rowman & Littlfield Publishers Inc.

International Development Law Organization [IDLO] and The Global Women's Institute. 2022. *Survivor-centered justice for gender-based violence in complex situations.* Retrieved 9 Mar 2023 at https://www.idlo.int/sites/default/files/2022/other/documets/survivor-centred_justice_for_sgbv_in_complex_situations.pdf.

Jackson, Sue. 2018. Young feminists, feminism and digital media. *Feminism & Psychology* 28 (1): 32–49.

Jewkes, Rachel, Jonathan Levin, and Loveday Penn-Kekana. 2002. Risk factors for domestic violence: Findings from a South African cross-sectional study. *Social Science & Medicine* 55 (9): 1603–1617.

Kaplan, Warren A. 2006. Can the ubiquitous power of mobile phones be used to improve health outcomes in developing countries? *Globalization and Health* 2 (1): 9. https://doi.org/10.1186/1744-8603-2-9.

Keller, Jessalynn. 2015. *Girls feminist blogging in a postfeminist age.* New York: Routledge.

Kelly, Liz. 1988. *Surviving sexual violence*. Minneapolis: University of Minnesota Press.

Kelly, Liz, and Jill Radford. 1998. Sexual violence against women and girls: An approach to an international overview. In *Thousand Oaks*, ed. Rethinking Violence Against. Women, E.W. Dobash, and R.P. Dobash, 53–76. CA: Sage Publicatons.

Kidman, Rachel. 2016. Child marriage and intimate partner violence: A comparative study of 34 countries. *International Journal of Epidemiology* 46 (2): 662–675.

Kim, Mimi E. 2011. Moving beyond critique: Creative interventions and reconstructions of community accountability. *Social Justice: A Journal of Crime Conflict & World Order* 37 (4): 14–35.

Magoga, Aldo. 2019. *Final evaluation: Eradicating violence against women and girls and improving access to justice for Maya rural women through culture-based community interventions*. New York: UN Women.

Martin, Betsan, and Jennifer Hand. 2006. Community responsibility for freedom from abuse. *Women's Studies Journal* 20 (1): 48–58.

Mendes, Kaitlynn, Jessalynn Keller, and Jessica Ringrose. 2018. Digitized narratives of sexual violence: Making sexual violence felt and known through digital disclosures. *New Media & Society* 21 (6): 1290–1310.

Merry, Sally Engle. 2006. *Human rights and gender violence: Translating international law into local justice*. Chicago and London: University of Chicago Press.

Minckas, Nicole, Geordan Shannon, and Jenevieve Mannell. 2020. The role of participation and community mobilization in preventing violence against women and girls: A programme review and critique. *Global Health Action* 13: 1–12. https://doi.org/10.1080/16549716.2020.1775061.

Mkandawire-Valhmu, Lucy, Claire Wendland, Patricia E. Stevens, Peninnah M. Kako, Anne Dressel, and Jennifer Kibicho. 2013. Marriage as a risk factor for HIV: Learning from the experiences of HIV-infected women in Malawi. *Global Public Health* 8(2):187–201.

New Haven/León Sister City Project. 2021. *Domestic violence prevention*. Retrieved 14 June 2024 at https://www.newhavenleon.org/domestic-violence-prevention.

Nikupeteri, Anna, Pia Skaffari, and Merja Laitinen. 2022. Feminist community work in preventing violence against women: A case study of addressing intimate partner violence in Finland. *Nordic Social Work Research* 12 (2): 256–269.

Nomamiukor, Faith O., and Blair E. Wisco. 2024. Social media's impact on rape myth acceptance and negative affect in college women: Examining the #MeToo and #HimToo movement. *Violence against Women* 30 (6–7): 1498–1516.

Núñez Puente, Sonia, Diana Fernández Romero, and Susana Vázquez Cupeiro. 2017. Online feminist practice, participatory activism and public policies against gender-based violence in Spain. *Feminist Theory* 18(3):299–321.

Núñez Puente, Sonia, Sergio D'Antonio Maceiras, and Diana Fernández Romero. 2021. Twitter activism and ethical witnessing: Possibilities and challenges of feminist politics against gender-based violence. *Social Science Computer Review* 39(2):295–311.

Oxfam. 2022. *Women watch group: It's never too late to contribute to women's empowerment.* Retrieved 15 June 2024 at https://philippines.oxfam.org/latest/image-story/women-watch-group-it%E2%80%99s-never-too-late-contribute-women%E2%80%99s-empowerment.

Pain, Paromita. 2021. 'It took me quite a long to develop a voice': Examining feminist digital activism in the Indian #MeToo movement. *News Media & Society* 23 (11): 3139–3155.

Putnam, Robert D. 2000. *Bowling Alone: The Collapse and Revival of American Community.* Simon & Schuster: New York, NY.

Raise Your Voice Saint Lucia, Inc. 2024. *Current projects: Agro Process Facility.* Retrieved 15 June 2024 at https://ryvslu.org/programs.

Renses, Pablo A., and Tanja Bosch. 2023. The limitations of hashtag feminist activism on South African twitter: A case study of #MenAreTrash and #WomenAreTrash. *Men and Masculinities* 26 (4): 585–603.

Rockflower. 2020. Partner portals: Foundation for women and children empowerment. Retrieved 16 June 2024 at https://www.rockflower.org/news/2020/4/15/foundation-for-women-and-children-empowerment.

Rockflower. 2024. *The five keys.* Retrieved 15 June 2024 at https://www.rockflower.org/the-five-key-program-areas.

Sabri, Bushra, Saraniya Tharmarajah, Veronica P.S. Njie-Carr, Jill T. Messing, Em Lowerzel, Joyell Arscott, and Jacquelyn C. Campbell. 2022. Safety planning with marginalized survivors of intimate partner violence: Challenges of conducting safety planning intervention research with marginalized women. *Trauma, Violence, & Abuse* 23(5):1728–1751.

Smith, Andrea. 2006. Beyond the politics of inclusion: Violence against women of color and human rights. *Meridians* 4 (2): 120–125.

Stern, Erin, and Lea Liliane Niyibizi. 2018. Shifting perceptions of consequences of IPV among beneficiaries of *Indashyikirwa*: An IPV prevention program in Rwanda. *Journal of Interpersonal Violence.* 33 (11): 1778–1804.

Sudderth, Lori K. 2015. Social networks in safety planning for victims of intimate partner violence: Community, battering, and safety. *Te Awatea Review* 12 (1): 2–5.

Sudderth, Lori K. 2020. The Women's project: Educating Women in Rural Nicaragua about gender and violence. *Affilia: Journal of Women and Social Work.* 35(2):246–259.

The CHAMPION Project. 2014. "Engaging men as partners: Promoting equitable gender norms through male engagement in Tanzania." *Champion Brief No. 2*. Dar es Salaam: EngenderHealth/CHAMPION Project.

United Nations Population Fund. 2009. *Partnering with men to end gender-based violence: Practices that work form Eastern Europe and Central Asia*. Retrieved 15 June 2024 at www.unfpa.org.

UN Women. 2013. *In brief: Ending violence against women and girls*. Retrieved 15 June 2024 https://www.unwomen.org/sites/default/files/Headqu arters/Attachments/Sections/Library/Publications/2013/12/UnWome nEVAW-ThemBrief_US-web-Rev9pdf.pdf.

Van der Kolk, Bessel. 2014. *The body keeps score: Brain, mind, and body in the healing of trauma*. New York City: Penguin Books.

White, R. and J. Zorza. 2010. *Safety plan for a friend, relative, or co-worker who is being abused by an intimate partner*. Domestic Violence Report Oct./Nov., 5–6.

Wilson, David and Shanda Kelsch. 2024. *Breaking the cycle: Empowering survivors of domestic abuse*. Presentation at Northeastern Academy of Criminal Justice Sciences, Gettysburg, PA. 7 June.

Women's Justice Initiative. 2024. *What we do*. Retrieved 15 June 2024 at https://womens-justice.org/what-we-do/.

Wood, Shannon N., Nancy Glass, and Michele R. Decker. 2021. An integrative review of safety strategies for women experiencing intimate partner violence in low- and middle-income countries. *Trauma, Violence, & Abuse* 22 (1): 68–82.

Woodlock, Delanie, Michael Salter, Molly Dragiewicz, and Bridget Harris. 2023. 'Living in darkness': Technology-facilitated coercive control, disenfranchised grief, and institutional betrayal. *Violence against Women* 29 (5): 987–1004.

World Bank. 2024. *World Bank Gender Strategy 2024–2030: Accelerate gender equality for a sustainable, resilient, and inclusive future—Consultation draft*. Washington: World Bank Group.

World Health Organization. 2022. *Violence studies: Prevention*. Retrieved 15 June 2024 at https://apps.who.int/violence-info/studies?area=intimate-par tner-violence&aspect=prevention&group-by=region.

INDEX

© The Editor(s) (if applicable) and The Author(s), under exclusive
license to Springer Nature Switzerland AG 2024
L. K. Sudderth, *Changing Communities in Challenging Contexts to
Address Intimate Partner Violence*,
https://doi.org/10.1007/978-3-031-75356-5

SPRINGER NATURE

GPSR Compliance

The European Union's (EU) General Product Safety Regulation (GPSR) is a set of rules that requires consumer products to be safe and our obligations to ensure this.

If you have any concerns about our products, you can contact us on ProductSafety@springernature.com

In case Publisher is established outside the EU, the EU authorized representative is:

Springer Nature Customer Service Center GmbH
Europaplatz 3
69115 Heidelberg, Germany

The manufacturer's authorised representative in the EU is Springer
Nature Customer Service Centre GmbH, Europaplatz 3, 69115 Heidelberg,
Germany. If you have any concerns regarding our products, please
contact ProductSafety@springernature.com

Printed and bound by CPI Group (UK) Ltd, Croydon, CR0 4YY
27/04/2026
02097607-0003